Paul Durkin

Moorland Grit

New routes and bouldering in
the North-West Peak District

PAUL DURKIN

MOORLAND GRIT
NEW ROUTES AND BOULDERING IN THE
NORTH-WEST PEAK DISTRICT

First published in 2021 by Dancing Gnome

Copyright @ Paul Durkin 2021

Paul Durkin has asserted his rights under the Copyright, Designs and Patents Act 1988 to be identified as author of this work.

A CIP catalogue record of this book is available from the British Library.

ISBN: 978-1-909461-57-4

All rights reserved. No part of this work covered by the copyright here-on may be reproduced or used in any form or by any means - graphic, electronic, or mechanised, including photocopying, recording, taping or information storage and retrieval systems - without the written permission of the publisher.

Typeset by Paul Durkin, Sheffield.

Printed and bound in the UK by Severn

Cover Photographs

Front cover

*Paul Durkin on first ascent of **The Prow**, E1 5b*
Whitegate Edge (Page 178)

Rear cover

Trepidation Buttress, Crow Stones, Derwent Valley

A Dancing Gnome production

Contents

Chapter	Title	Page
Foreword		1
Acknowledgements		4
1	Bottoms Quarry	7
2	Broad Mills Buttresses	19
3	Bull Stones	21
4	Coombes Clough Outcrops	25
5	Coombes Rocks	29
6	Cowbury Dale	48
7	Cown Edge Rocks and Altar Quarry	62
8	Crook Hill	71
9	Crow Stones	75
10	Crowden Great Brook, Shield and Easter Buttresses	82
11	Dovestones Boulders	84
12	Doctor's Gate Circuit	91
12.1	Lower Right Shelf Stones	93
12.2	Higher Shelf Stones	94
12.3	In Between Shelf Stones	96
12.4	Lower Left Shelf Stones	97
12.5	James's Thorn	98
12.6	Near Ashton Clough	99
13	Photographs	103
14	Ironbower Rocks	108
15	Longdendale Trail Rocks	112
16	Long Gutter Edge	117
17	Middle Black Clough	118

18	Mount Famine	123
19	The Naze	127
20	Ogden Clough	130
21	Oldpits Quarry Boulder and Edge	138
22	Park Bridge	140
23	Swan Clough Quarry	142
24	Tintwistle Knarr Outcrop	145
25	Torside Naze	147
26	Woodhead Tunnel Rocks	148
27	Near Yellowslacks	155

Kirklees Area — 158

28	Bilberry Reservoir Slab	159
29	Holme Moss	162
30	Marsden Clough	164
31	Ramsden Clough	169
32	White Gate Edge	175

Index — 183

Maps

Map 1.1:	Quarries, Edges and Bouldering Locations (North)	2
Map 1.2:	Quarries, Edges and Bouldering Locations (South)	3
Map 7.1:	Cown Edge Rocks and Altar Quarry	63
Map 12.1:	Doctor's Gate Circuit - Location Map	92
Map 27.1:	Kirklees Edges and Rocks	158

Photographs

Photo 3.1: Paul Durkin on **Frog's mouth** 4c, Bull Stones — 24
Photo 5.1: Paul Durkin, **Audacity**, VS 5a * first ascent — 37
Photo 5.2: Simon Royston **Not For T'Short**, E1 5b * first ascent — 43
Photo 13.1: Malcolm Baxter, **Sniffle,** first ascent E1 5b *, Marsden Clough — 103
Photo 13.2: Malcolm Baxter, **Bloodstain**, 5b *, Lower Right Shelf Stones — 104
Photo 13.3: Simon Troop, **No Country for Old Men**, E2 5c, Cowbury Dale — 105
Photo 13.4: Adrienn Angyal, **Two Up, One Across** VS 5a*, Altar Quarry — 106
Photo 13.5: Simon Royston, first ascent **Oroxylum Indicum**, E1 6a — 107
Photo 26.1: Paul Durkin on first ascent of **Permanent Way**, E1 5b* — 150
Photo 26.2: Malcolm Baxter, 1st ascent of **Out of Your Signal Box**, E2 5c* — 152
Photo 30.1: Paul Durkin, **S'not Bad,** HVS 5b* first ascent, Marsden Clough — 168
Photo 32.1: Simon Royston on **Awesome Wells** E2 6a, first ascent — 179

Foreword

There's lots of rock in the north west Peak District such as Tintwistle Knarr, Laddow, Hobson Moor Quarry and of course, just over the hill, Chew Valley, where climbers go to get their guide book ticks. The 'Over The Moors' BMC guide covered most of the grit that abounds in the peak, but the more discerning climber may wish to be a bit more adventurous and a little more esoteric in their outlook. This is for them - come and visit some lesser-known sites near to Glossop (and some a little bit further afield).

Malcolm (Malc) Baxter, a well-known climber around Glossop, had listed the location of these little-known crags and quarries since he started climbing in the 1950s, and tramped ceaselessly around Glossop and surrounds on this quest, sometimes followed by apprentices both young and old. A flurry of checking these routes, and more than a few new ones as well, in the last few years has resulted in a worthy collection of problems and routes to explore and enjoy. Those whose grade limit is E2 should relish this guide, as that's the hardest listed in these pages bar one E3 route at Bottoms Quarry (nothing over 6a as well except one F7b at Crook Hill). The grades are all British, with stars awarded by the authors.

So, for those that are tempted, a veritable feast of routes and problems have been looked at. Some were climbed, some were looked at again puzzlingly or identified for better climbers than us! The results are presented in this (hopefully useful) guide. This was despite a suggestion made by one 'friend', who will remain nameless (and who'd not been to any of the crags), that to accompany Ken Wilson's series of books, this should perhaps be christened 'Shite Rock'. Our wanderings may highlight the natural curiosity of climbers to check out every bit of rock. Could this then be the start of the Peak District 'esoteric' tick list? It is certain that some of these sites rank with many other rocks in the county (honest!). Try visiting these spots first and see whether the accolade is deserved, or proved unfounded. Hopefully this will produce a rash of enthusiasm for these more remote spots and a desire for further exploration - there's certainly opportunities for filling in gaps (though we think they're small gaps!).

Please shout up if you disagree with the grades and send the author any information on new ones.

Please send details (and dynamic colourful photographs if possible) to paul.durkin11@gmail.com or send snail mail to 9 Mercia Drive, Dore, Sheffield, S17 3QF.

Paul Durkin, March 2021.

Crag Map

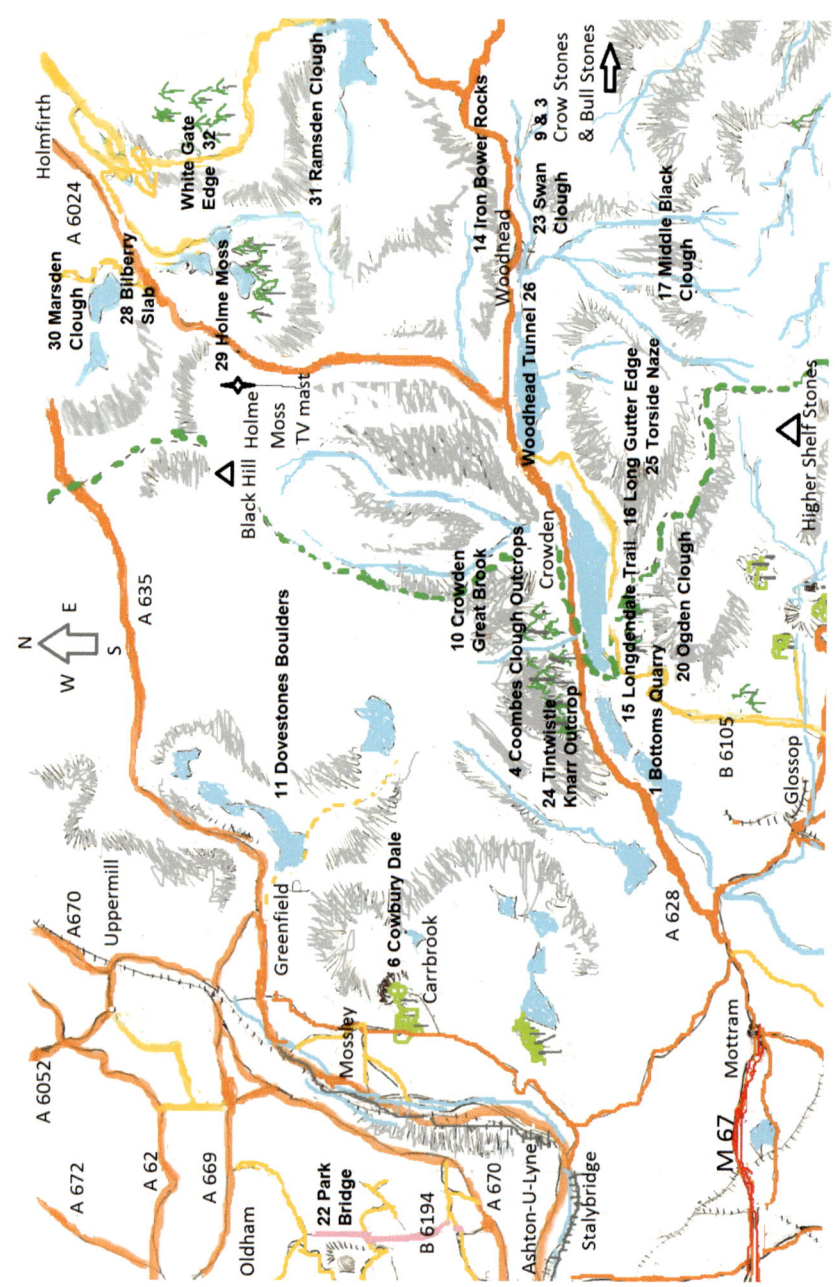

Map 1.1: Quarries, Edges and Bouldering Locations (North)

Crag Map

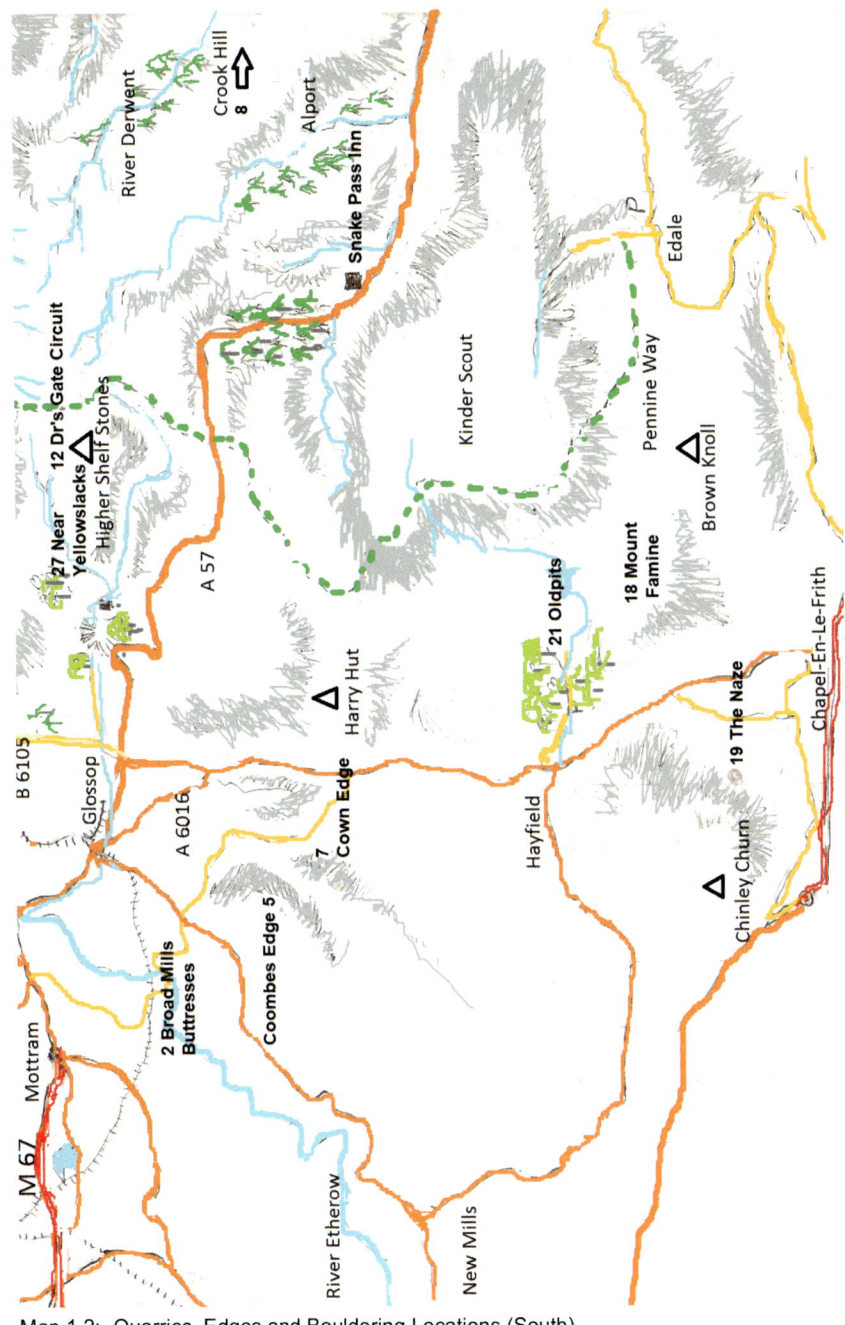

Map 1.2: Quarries, Edges and Bouldering Locations (South)

Acknowledgements

Every effort has been made to achieve accuracy in the information in this guidebook. The author, publishers and copyright owner can take no responsibility for loss or injury to persons; loss or damage to property or equipment; trespass; irresponsible behaviour or any other mishap that may be suffered because of following descriptions or advice offered in this guidebook. The inclusion of a crag or quarry or bouldering area does not guarantee a right to climb there or a Right of Way to reach it.

As some of these quarries are seldom visited, owls and peregrines have been observed or reported as using the ledges as nesting sites. During the nesting season, please exercise good judgement so as not to disturb a nest. Some common indicators of nest disturbance are:

- Alarm calling
- Visibly agitated birds, sometimes circling the threat
- Mock or actual dive bombing

If climbers observe behaviour of this kind (or any other obvious signs of disturbance) from birds at the crag, the best advice is to back off until the birds stop displaying signs of distress. If this occurs whilst at the base of the crag, this is easy enough, but if it happens mid-climb, back off as soon as is safely possible.

Grading System

We have been traditionally British about the grades (all three of us are of that era) except for one line on Crook Hill done by others at F7b. For more modern climbers the comparison between traditional grit and French grades is approximately:

British	4a	4b	4c	5a	5b	5c		6a		6b	
French	F3	F4	F4+	F5	F5+	F6a	F6a+	F6b	F6b+	F6c	F6c+	F7a	F7a+	F7b

Now the formal stuff's out of the way, let's crack on. The original interest was just to climb, the concept of this guide book came later. This has been a labour of love, pushed to fruition by Malcolm Baxter, Simon Royston and the author. We've also been assisted by guest climbers from time to time. The three of us did more digging than you can throw a shovel at, spent lengthy periods dangling in harnesses with numb legs and eyefuls of dust, oh, and yes, some climbing. But there've been so many laughs, and more laughs, so much so that even cleaning in the rain was fun (yes, we are mad!).

Thanks to the following climbers, photographers, proof readers, checkers and others (not forgetting our partners for letting us go out to play) who've helped to successfully publish this book.

(In alphabetical order)

Rick Adderton	Dolores Durkin
Adrienn Angyal	Iain Johnson
Eileen Baxter	Lois McGrath
Jack Christian	Matt 'Jo' Rhodes
Nick Corbett	Sam Whiting

Which rocks to include?

The choice of where to climb was influenced by 'The Rules'. There were only three of them - not many - but important. Simon framed them early on and got no objections from the other two. So... the rules - well, in no particular order they are:

- Not in a book yet
- Not likely to meet anybody else, either on the way to, or at the crag
- No one goes there

So, when we started, the choice of which crags and edges seemed pretty straight forward - it was the list compiled by Malc, wasn't it? All the crags and edges happily satisfied all three of the rules... happy days! The intention was to include all the small crags around Glossop that most people had never heard of or had generally ignored. Well, that's how it was at first, but it grew….and it grew! And then grew some more.

There was always another small quarry or edge that 'really needed to be included', and so it was.

Then one day Malc contacted the outside world - well, Kirklees to be precise - and thought it'd be good to include all their crags as well! Once we'd soundly emphasised to Malc that this was a step too far, he agreed to come down to earth again and concentrate on 'what's really needed'. That didn't last long - he'd spotted a crag that 'no-one had climbed', and 'it really needed to be in the book'. This was the thin end of the wedge - the door was opened. So, in order, those that slipped through were Ramsden Edge, White Gate Edge, Marsden Clough, Bilberry Reservoir slab and Holme Moss. Marsden Clough turned out to be one of the most pleasant crags to climb on in beautiful surroundings - what more to wish for!

If you remember that the first rule was 'Not in a book'; you might notice that some of the edges and quarries have already been included in the 2012 'Over The Moors' (OTM) guide or the down-loads on the BMC website. Well, they did fit the rule until we submitted them to the BMC. We have

Acknowledgements

repeated them here because OTM only included limited text and some first ascent information was left out. Our versions include full descriptions and more detailed first ascents lists. Some additional routes have also been climbed and added since OTM was published.

Meet the Team

Just in case you see any of us in the street, or at a climbing wall, and you want to congratulate us for introducing you to such a good read, we are:

Malc Baxter
Source: David Price

Paul Durkin
Source: Simon Royston

Simon Royston
Source: Paul Durkin

1 Bottoms Quarry

Paul Durkin
OS ref. SK029973   alt. 180m

This gem of a quarry should be added to your list of favourite places. It sits above Bottoms Reservoir, the lowermost of five storage reservoirs within Woodhead Pass. The quarry generally comprises sound fine grained gritstone some 200m long characterised by sharp edges and crack lines, varying in height from 5m to 17m. The majority of the rock gets lots of sun and is quick to dry out.

Conditions and aspect: Lots of sun through most of the day with only two faces losing the sun in late morning - good for those hot afternoons. The quarry faces South South East, and has only slight seepage. **Routes and bouldering:** 53 routes from Mod to E3. No specific bouldering but smaller routes could be treated as such. Belays at the tops are generally good providing cams are carried. **Parking and approach:** Vehicular access is from the A628(T) opposite Chapel Brow, Tintwistle. A tarmac road leads down the hill until after some 450m the quarry gate can be seen on the left. Parking for 4 cars in a gateway on the right 15m past the gate. Be considerate as this gate provides access for a local angling club. Two minutes from car to the first climb. **Access:** The quarry is owned by United Utilities and you may be asked to leave - there's no agreement in place for climbers.

1.   Tottering Tower VS 5a   2008
9m   The left side of the arête through the aptly named top section. Tree belay 4m back.

2.   Bashful VS 4c   2008
5m   Start beneath the recess, go directly to the top - better than it looks.
3.   Grumpy VS 5a   2008
5m   The middle of the wall very pleasantly to the top.
4.   Sneezy VS 4c   2008
5m   From below the right slanting overhanging groove without deviation.
5.   Sleepy VS 4c   1960s
5m   Start 2m right below a crack at 2/3rds height and head straight up.
6.   Doc VS 4c   2008
5m   At the right end of the black wall, climb the left side of the arête.

The pocketed roof to the right may provide entertainment for the gymnasts. The five routes to the right of the descent route have little or no protection and are probably best soloed.

7.   Black Edge Left Hand Mod   1960s
5m   The easy ledges immediately on the right to join the top part of the descent route.
8.   Black Edge VS 5a   1960s
5m   The overhanging arête immediately on the right of the descent route past an ancient iron hook.
9.   Yellow Wall E1 5b   1960s
5m   A quality problem - pull through the overhang on sharp pockets to good holds.

10. Yellow Wall Right-Hand VS 4c 2008
7m   Just right and 1m left of the right arête, pull through a slight groove in the overhanging wall.

11. Quality Street VS 4c *   1960s
7m   The left side of the arête is climbed pleasantly to the top.
12. Pluto HVS 5b *   2009
7m   The arête on its right side steeply to the top.
13. Uranus E2 5c *   2008
7m   The centre of the steep wall, gain a sharp flake on the right before boldly launching either up, or, left via a small flake to gain the top.
14. The Third Half E3 6a   2008
8m   The wall 5m right has only been top roped. Pass the 'tooth' to gain an edge and then rock over to a l-o-n-g reach up and left. Move up and then back right to a pocket and a hard finish left of the overhanging blocks.
15. Wren's Corner VS 4c   2008
8m   The corner just right. Finish at the ledge on the right at HS, or continue left to finish in an airy position between two overhanging blocks.

16. Battle of the Bulge E2 5b * 2009
6m Start just right of the corner, move up and right before gaining a good hold, past poor pockets to better holds above. For the tall the bottom section can be taken direct, reducing the route's strenuousness. Don't bother looking for gear placements - there aren't any until the top!

17. Satisfaction Guaranteed S 4b * 2007
7m The obvious crack 3m from the right arête just left of a large block.

18. Betwixt and Between VS 5a 2008
7m Between the crack and the arête climb the centre of the block and the wall above without recourse to the LH crack other than for protection. Give yourself an E1 tick without the protection.

19. Waterloo Sunset HS, 4b * 2007
7m Climb the arête pleasantly on its left side to the large ledge.

20. Spike Arête HVS 5b * 2008
7m Up the wall just right of the arête passing between two spikes.

21. Autumn Almanac VS 4c 2007
7m Starting 2m right of the arête climb the cracks and head for the notch in the top

Bottoms Quarry

22.　Lola　VS 5a　　　　　　　　　　　　　　　　　　2007
7m　Start below and between two square holes, climb the cracks straight up and left.

23.　Ranger's Return　VS, 4c　　　　　　　　　　　　2008
7m　The wall 1m left of the corner heading for an oak near the top.

24.　Parta the Strata　E1 5b *　　2008
8m　Attain a position on the (detached?) block, up to the break and then a pocket via the short arête.

25.　Letterbox Crack　HVS 5b　　　　　　　　　　　1995
8m　Up the slab to the crack in the headwall. Go leftwards via a large pocket, or slightly easier, make a tricky move up the crack.

26.　Postman's Craic　VS 4c　　　　　　　　　　　　2008
8m　Easy ledges beneath, and heading for, a niche at the top. A challenging finish for VS leaders.

27. Magic Bramble HVS 5a 2008
8m From the RH side of the ledge, straight up and through the overlaps.

28. Sunny Delight HVS 4c 2008
8m Good crack climbing to the small left facing corner, sparse protection.

*The next four routes start from the same ledge - gained at a square notch at **Severe** grade, continued above by:*

29. Hearts S 2008
8m From the ledge go left on easy steps.

30. Clubs HS 4b 2008
8m The left side of the wall gaining a pocket just before the top.

31. Diamonds VS 5a 2008
8m The white streak through the overhang and steep wall above. The short need not apply!

32. Spades S 4b 2008
8m Pleasantly up the right arête on good holds.

33. No Trumps VS 4c   2009
8m   The groove and wall above.

34. Pinwheel VS 4c   2008
6m   The wall up to the curving flake and the crack above.

35. Catherine Wheel HVS 5b *   2008
6m   Right side of the arête then left at the break past the pulley wheel.

36. Aperitif VS 4c   2008
7m   The corner to the right.

37. Entrée HVS 5b   2008
6m   The middle of the wall to the top.

38. Simple Fare D   2008
6m   From the right end of the platform move easily up good ledges.

39. Just Desert D   2008
6m   The arête via ledges.

40. Long Buttress V Diff   2010
12m   Unfortunately spoilt by the loose rock near the top - time and traffic should improve it.

41. Tall Man's Arête VS 5a 2010
7m Gain the ledge by a hard move at 4m, continue behind the tree.
42. Sandstorm VS 4c 2010
13m Up to the buttress which is climbed left of centre to easier ledges above. Tree belay 4m back.
43. Allegedly S 4b 2010
13m Start 1m right and go up the series of ledges.
44. Stacked Arête S 4b 2010
5m Pleasantly up the lower rocks and then on the right side of the arête.

Further right again is a large 15m high section. The interlocked blocks over Damocles' Boulders are quite scary - notwithstanding this, the line gives one of the most enjoyable routes in the quarry.

45. Bruised HVS 5c   2014
6m   The crack in the overhanging wall to a good ledge and a solid cam runner before the mantelshelf which is much harder than it looks!

46. Syracuse VS 4c   2014
15m Climb the corner to the small ledge at 3m, move to its left end, step up and left to gain the large ledge. Take the headwall on the left.

47. Damocles' Boulders VS 5a   2008
15m The corner until a move right to the arête can be made continuing easily up the blocks above.

48. Dionysius E1 6a   2014
15m An eliminate line up the overhanging nose, first on the right before stepping up and left with a hard move to stand up (without bridging left). Continue upwards on small footholds, staying on the left side of the arête. Take the easy upper arête directly.

49. Oroxylum Indicum E1 6a   2014

15m From the shelf on the right go left up the wall to the break (crux) and a step left to the arête. Step back right and continue up the blocks above. Harder for people shorter than 1.93m/6ft 4in.

50. Hollow Flake E1 5b *   2009

15m From the shelf climb the crack boldly rightwards to the hanging flake and better holds. From the top of the flake move left to share the top section with Damocles' Boulders.

51. Fruitcake HVD   2014

15m The groove between the two oak trees, continuing on the left side of the large niche, wondering how the rock is still there.

52. Kylie HVS 5b *   2014

18m Right of the previous climb, scramble down rubble to a point directly below the highest point of the quarry. Climb ledges on the left side of the pillar until a hard move to gain the right side then enables a

thankful jam to be reached. Pull up, continue on the right side of the large ledge before hard moves up the wall using pockets and a welcome top.

53. Sunstroke HVS 5a   2014
18m 2m right of the previous route, climb steps trending right to achieve a stance on the pillar. Step up before heading left to a pocket and up the wall to a finishing jug.

****

First Ascents

1960s	**Sleepy, Black Edge, Yellow Wall, Quality Street** Malc Baxter solo
1995 Feb	**Letterbox Crack** Malcolm Baxter, Matthew Rhodes
2007 Oct	**Lola** Paul Durkin, Malcolm Baxter, Matthew Rhodes
	Waterloo Sunset Matthew Rhodes solo
	Autumn Almanac Malcolm Baxter, Paul Durkin
	Satisfaction Guaranteed Malcolm Baxter, Paul Durkin, Matthew Rhodes
2008 May	**Uranus, Spike Arête** Paul Durkin, Malcolm Baxter
2008 June	**Catherine Wheel** Paul Durkin, Malcolm Baxter
	Letterbox Crack Malcolm Baxter, Paul Durkin Direct finish
	Ranger's Return Malcolm Baxter, Paul Durkin *Named for the Park Ranger who asked 'what were we doing' and 'did we know we shouldn't be there!'*
2008 June	**Betwixt and Between** Paul Durkin, Malcolm Baxter
	The Third Half Rick Adderton top roped
	Yellow Wall Right-Hand Ian Johnson solo
2008 July	**Parta the Strata** Malcolm Baxter, Paul Durkin *Malc led 90% of the route before expiring at a red herring finish involving a horrendous, energy-sapping under-cling. His second then led the route, climbing the finish just slightly left of Malc's titanic struggles after discovering a hitherto obscured small hold on the arête.*
2008 Aug	**Sneezy, Doc, Tottering Tower, Magic Bramble** Paul Durkin, Malcolm Baxter *Magic Bramble was named for the seemingly everlasting root pulled from a crack while cleaning.*
	Wren's Corner, Postman's Craic Malcolm Baxter, Paul Durkin
	Bashful Malc Baxter, Paul Durkin and Simon Royston
	Grumpy Paul Durkin, Malc Baxter and Simon Royston
2008 Aug	**Simple Fare** Malcolm Baxter solo
2008 Sept	**Sunny Delight, Aperitif,** Paul Durkin, Malcolm Baxter
	Pinwheel Malcolm Baxter, Paul Durkin

	Entrée Paul Durkin solo
	Just Desert Malcolm Baxter solo
2008 Oct	**Damocles' Boulders** Paul Durkin, Malcolm Baxter
	Diamonds Malcolm Baxter, Paul Durkin
	Hearts Malcolm Baxter solo
	Clubs, Spades Paul Durkin solo
2009 June	**Battle of the Bulge, No Trumps** Paul Durkin solo
	Hollow Flake Paul Durkin, Malcolm Baxter
	Pluto Malcolm Baxter, Paul Durkin
2009 July	**Bruised** Paul Durkin top roped (led by S Royston 3 May 2014)
2010 Oct	**Long Buttress, Allegedly** Malc Baxter, Paul Durkin, Simon Royston
	Tall Man's Arête Simon Royston solo
2011 March	**Sandstorm, Stacked Arête** Simon Royston, Paul Durkin, Malc Baxter
2014 April	**Oroxylum Indicum** Simon Royston, Paul Durkin, Malc Baxter
	We only went back to the quarry to try and lead Bruised, but having tried and failed we looked at the arête as a consolation. After a bit of cleaning, we all tried before Royston managed the tricky balance and a reachy move to add this excellent route.
2014 May	**Dionysius** Paul Durkin, Simon Royston, Malc Baxter
	Spurred on by Royston's success on Oroxylum Indicum, *Durkin looked at an alternative start, before realising that an independent line could possibly be made by staying left of the arête. A few trial moves on the arête were made before aching muscles demanded a pint in The Crown in Glossop. The route was led successfully the following week to give a fine route. Another attempt by Durkin to lead* Bruised *failed, but Royston, despite declaring that 'it wasn't his type of route', then eased his way to success.*
2014 June	**Kylie** Simon Royston, Paul Durkin, Malc Baxter
	Route cleaning and a significant bramble clearing exercise below the highest part of the quarry proved to be worth the effort. One of the best of Bottoms - hence the name!
2014 June 22	**Fruitcake** Malc Baxter, Paul Durkin
	Sunstroke Paul Durkin, Malc Baxter

2 Broad Mills Buttresses

Paul Durkin
OS ref. SJ 992 937 alt. 115m

These two buttresses are 300m northwest of the heritage site of Broad Mills. From the brambles, soil and grass removed during cleaning it's doubtful whether the routes had been climbed previously. Worth a visit, not least to get the esoteric tick.

Conditions and aspect: Situated immediately adjacent to the north bank of the River Etherow, comprising sandy gritstone with great river views.
Routes: The first buttress has three climbs, the second buttress some 50m west has a further three routes. **Parking and approach:** Turn south off Market Street, Broadbotton, into Lymefield and park at Lymefield Visitor Centre. Follow the path west through the mill site, signposted 'Hodgefold', past the footbridge, to the end of Well Row, a stone-built terrace. Continue west up the path, still signed 'Hodgefold' for 40m until just past the brow a descent can be made on the left to the first buttress. **Access:** No problem. Please do not park at the end of Well Row.

1. **Caterpillar Wall** E1 5b. 2011
6m Climb up and left heading for a blocky hold and a finish at the terrace (micro wire up and right). Short but good.

2. **Caterpillar Rib** S 4b 2011
6m Three metres right gain the terrace using the wall and rib.

3. **Caterpillar Crack** VS 4c 2011
14m The bulge to the crack and rib above to a ledge and tree at 9m, possible belay. Move right 2m and up the short wide crack to another ledge and then the top left of the block.

The second buttress is best approached by the path leading west from the top of the first buttress. 50m along the path is a large oak tree with twin trunks 3m left of the path - the buttress is directly below. Best to abseil from the tree. For the adventurous it is possible to traverse the steep hillside at river level from the first buttress to the second.

The bottom 3m is on questionable rock - don't be put off, all three routes are worthwhile.

4.   Acorner S 4b   2011
11m Start left of the corner below a square groove, surmount the bulge (crux), up the wall and crack above.

5.   Wimper & Cringe E1 5a   2011
11m The groove, moving right at 3m to the ledge. Challenging moves up the left arête and wall on dubious wires. Better, and harder, than it looks.

6.   Three Happy Ducks VS 4c 2011
11m From the ledge take a line up the front right of the buttress to the oak tree. Good climbing with the crux at the top, though the first runner may be worryingly high for some.

****

First Ascents
2011 May   **Caterpillar Wall** Paul Durkin, Malc Baxter, Simon Royston
Caterpillar Rib Simon Royston solo
Caterpillar Crack Simon Royston, Paul Durkin, Malc Baxter, Iain Johnson
2011 June   **Wimper & Cringe** Paul Durkin, Malc Baxter, Simon Royston
Acorner Malc Baxter, Paul Durkin, Simon Royston
Three Happy Ducks Simon Royston, Paul Durkin, Malc Baxter

3 Bull Stones

Paul Durkin
OS ref. SK 179962   alt. 480m

The stones comprise good quality moorland grit, has probably been climbed on before but we've been unable to find any records of any routes or problems. The edge consists of a group of buttresses and boulders seemingly tipped from a giant's toy box. The stones are sound, clean, coarse-grained gritstone with problems and routes varying in length from 3m to 6m. The rock enjoys the sun most of the day and is quick to dry. None of the routes are particularly high in the technical grades but the situation and quality of climbs make it a good day out in cracking surroundings.

Conditions and aspect: Lots of sun throughout the day. The edge is largely south facing with fantastic views across the Derwent Valley to the south and Bleaklow to the west. **Routes and bouldering:** 17 routes and problems from Mod to 5c. The lines are largely boulder problems but there are a number of lines for which you may wish to use a rope. **Parking and approach:** Vehicular access is from the south from the A57 at Ladybower, **Access:** The buttresses are in open countryside on CRoW land.

From the A57 take the turnoff to the Derwent Valley, then go 2.5 miles north to the visitor centre at Fairholmes. You have two alternatives - on Mondays to Fridays continue northwards for another 6 miles to Kings Tree where parking is available at the bus turnaround, or, at weekends when the road to Kings Tree is closed, park at Fairholmes, or one of the free parking areas before reaching Fairholmes, and catch the 222 bus to King's Tree. The service operates on Saturdays and Sundays and originates at Bamford Station starting at 08:45 - beware, the last bus leaves Kings Tree at 17:15 (times are correct for 2013 - please check for the current timetable). From King's Tree, follow the track north to Slippery Stones and cross the 17th century pack horse bridge which was relocated in 1959 from the now flooded valley. Continue north for a further half mile to reach a fork at the junction with the Cut Gate bridleway. There are 2 ways from here - left or right. Either take the left fork for a further 800m and then the right fork up the clough. Follow this until reaching the 500m contour where a clearly marked path runs between Crow Stones and Bull Stones. Follow the track right to the easily visible Bull Stones. An hour and 20 minutes from King's Tree.

Alternatively, at the junction with the Cut Throat bridleway, go right up the bridleway - Follow this for about 1 mile until you reach a large cairn. Turn left here and follow the path which contours around to the stones. This is also an hour and 20 minutes from King's Tree.

Climbs are described left to right and start with a problem at the left (west) end on a block in front of the main group, and one final (no. 17) on the east.

1. **Starter** 5b 2013
3m A little artificial as you can't use the right arête.
The arête to the left of the next route had chalk on it on the day we visited the crag. We couldn't do anything with it, but somebody may have done.
2. **Warm Up** 4b 2013
3. **Step Up** 4b 2013
5m On the right side of the leaning blocks up the centre of the slab 2013
4. **Wall** 4c 2013
5. **Wall Like** 4c 2013
6. **Frustrated** 5c 2013
7. **Braced and a Bit** 4c 2013
8. **Crack'n Edge** 4c 2013
9. **Double Edged** 4c 2013
6m Excellent - up the middle of the blocks with the crux at the top
10. **Slant** 5a 2013
6m Use the wall left of the arête before stepping left and up the front of the three blocks. The middle section can be taken on its right at the same grade before moving left to take the top block directly up the front.

11.	**Wedge Wall** 4b	2013
12.	**Piece of Cake** mod	2013
13.	**Nearly a Slab** 4b	2013
14.	**Frog's Mouth** 4c	2013

15.	**Toad's Mouth** 4c	2013
16.	**Watch Out!** 5b	2013

Be careful if tempted to solo, it's a horrible landing, and the crux is getting over the top.

Some 25m further to the right is

17.	**Escape** 4c	2013

Photo 3.1: Paul Durkin on **Frog's mouth** 4c, Bull Stones

Source: Malc Baxter

First Ascents

All recorded routes were climbed by Malc Baxter and Paul Durkin over two visits in August 2013. Given the chalk found on the second visit, we can't lay claim to any of them being firsts - just first recorded (as far as we know!).

4 Coombes Clough Outcrops

Malc Baxter
OS refs. SK 053 998, SK 055 995, SK 057 995 alt. 500m

Two isolated outcrops, close together and a small bouldering area approximately 0.5 km SE of the northerly rocks, all of which are seldom visited. The northerly rocks are identified on the map as Lad's Leap. They are near the head of the clough on the right ascending.

Conditions and aspect: The northerly crag is of a more brittle rock which contrasts with the southerly outcrop of weathered moorland gritstone. Great moorland views. **Routes:** The northerly rocks have currently got six climbs with scope for more. The nearby southerly crags are suitable for beginners and for soloing easier climbs, though only one climb is identified. 7 problems have been recorded on rocks approximately 0.5 km SE from the head of the clough. **Parking and approach:** Park at Crowden and follow paths past the Youth Hostel and up onto the edge of Rakes Moss Moor heading west to the head of the clough. Just after a large cairn where the path crosses the stream, head down it, veering left to beneath the northerly rocks. Time to the crag one hour. **Access:** No problem - it's CRoW access land.

Coombes Clough North, SK 053 998
The first route lies on the west side of the stream on the biggest buttress.

1.   Deadleg HVS 5a   2014
6m   The centre of the buttress up the wide crack which is not as easy as it looks - a climb worth seeking out.

Back to the east bank for the following

2.   Cape Verde S 4b   2014
7m   The arête, with the crux at the bottom.

3.   Brace and Bit E1 5c *   2013
7m   Start in the centre of the wall at the arête. Climb a short layback crack. Step left to a small foothold and make a move up before stepping back to the centre of the wall. Reach the top by small crimps and footholds which you'd like to be bigger (crux). Small / micro wires needed.

4.   Africa Wall E1 5a   2008
7m   The arête all the way to the top, starting on the right and then the left. An alternative (original) start is up the crack of Brace and Bit before stepping right to the arête.

5.   Sicily S 4b   2014
7m   The arête first on its right before moving to its left.

6.   Corsican Bandit HVS 5a   2014
7m   The short steep crack to reach the ledge. Now the fun bit to achieve a standing position. Continue up the centre of the wall.

Coombes Clough Edge, OS Ref. SK 055 995

This is just south of the previous rocks and consists of a naturally weathered gritstone edge which can be climbed on nearly everywhere at 'v diff' standard, the best being the buttress at the right-hand end (B2) and a buttress near the centre (B1), some 30m apart. The right side of B1 has repulsed all attempts to climb it without the left arête, and the left arête on its right is 5a. (Malc Baxter 19 October 2007).

Coombes Clough Right OS Ref. SK 057 995

This is a small cluster of rocks about 0.5km south east of the Coombes Clough Rocks. It is best found by following a wall from the top path. The wall veers left (facing out) at SK 060 998 to descend the moor. Before it

steepens, go left to these rocks. The wall continues down to "Round Hill Rocks" which contain two climbs, the best being *Sweepsearch* VS 4c up the tower. Coombes Clough Right can also be found by going some 0.5 km SE from the head of Coombes Clough contouring round the moor edge.

1. 4b Right edge of block
2. 4b Straight up the centre through the overlap
3. 5a Step off a block onto the slab, going either left or right avoiding the arêtes (interestingly, there is good shelter behind this slab).
4. 5b The wall using both arêtes
5. 5a The projecting flake and crack
6. 5a The undercut direct up the centre
7. 5a Up through the little roof

****

First Ascents

2008 Feb	**Africa Wall** Iain Johnson, Malc. Baxter	
2013 Sept	**Brace and Bit** Paul Durkin, Malc Baxter	
2014 Aug	**Deadleg** Malc Baxter, Simon Royston	
	Cape Verde Simon Royston solo	
2014 Sept	**Sicily** Paul Durkin, Malc Baxter	
	Corsican Bandit Malc Baxter, Paul Durkin	
2014 Aug	Coombes Clough Right - Malc Baxter, Simon Royston	

5 Coombes Rocks

Paul Durkin
OS ref SK017916   alt. 390m

This partially quarried edge above Charlesworth has until recently been sadly neglected because of access restrictions - signs stating 'Danger', 'Private', and 'Keep Off' are liberally daubed all over. The CRoW Act now allows exploration and some excellent routes were uncovered (and one or two re-discovered). The edge is mentioned in John Laycock's 1913 book 'Some Shorter Climbs (In Derbyshire and Elsewhere)'. The rock comprises numerous gritstone buttresses stretching for over 1000m, characterised by sharp edged and sloping breaks and tops with steep and often overhanging faces. The bouldering and climbs vary from 4m to 13m. The rocks were included in *Over The Moors*, but since then an additional 8 climbs have been done at the southern end.

Conditions and aspect: The curving edge faces west at its north end and north west at the southern. The rocks get the afternoon sun with some of the bays becoming sun traps later in the day. Care must be taken with some of the tops which can be dusty and loose. **Routes and bouldering:** 64 routes from HVD to E1 including 15 bouldering problems. **Parking and approach:** From the A624 heading south from Glossop turn right at the top of the hill into Monk's Road and follow the road for some 2.5km before cresting the hill and parking immediately on the right in a lay-by (see the map on page 63). Alternatively, from Glossop Road, Charlesworth take Town Lane (opposite the George & Dragon) and Chapel Brow (signposted as 'Hayfield 4m') which then becomes Monk's Road, up the hill to park in the same lay-by, which is now on your left. Cross the road some 75m down the hill from the lay-by, through a gate (and if you're feeling silly, over the totally unnecessary stile) followed by a pleasant amble across the field along the sunken track. The first buttress is some 50m away from the gate in the sunken track. 7 minutes from car to edge. **Access:** The edge lies on two farms, but it is on CRoW land.

Northern End, First Bay

1.   Portside Arête 4c   2010
5m   The steep arête mainly on the left side.
2.   Cave Route Left 5a   2010
5m   The left side of the cave.
3.   Green Wall 5b   2010
5m   Avoid the alarmingly hollow bottom of the green flake.
4.   Cave Route Right 5a   2010
5m   Pass the hole on its left
5.   Starboard Arête 4a   2010
5m   The easy arête.
6.   Short Wall 4c   2010
4m   Innocuous but worthwhile.
7.   Arête and Wall 4c   2010
4m   As it says!
8.   Another Wall 4c   2010
4m   Up the middle

Cave Route Right: Paul Durkin

Eccles Cake Wall: Simon Royston

The back wall of the First Bay is steep and overhanging

9. Staircase 4c   2010
5m Pleasantly up the walls.

10. Nostril 5a   2010
5m Up the nose, continuing up the wall behind.

11. Left(ish) Wall 5a 2010
5m The wall left of the crack.

12. Crack and Nose 5a 2010
5m The crack going over the nose at the top.

13. The Shelf 5b 2010
5m Achieving a standing position on the shelf is harder than it looks

14. Flaky Cracks 5a 2010
4m Up the wall between the two cracks.

15. Right(ish) Wall 5a 2010
4m Short but steep.

The next significant bay is some 50m southwards just after a small square bay containing a dry-stone retaining wall at its rear.

Second Bay

The overhanging buttress at the northern end of the bay is imposing and a bit scary! The whole of the front section seems to be about to fall off - but don't think about it too much - it has been there a long time.

16.   Audacity VS 5a * 2010
6m   The steep wall to the roof, take a deep breath, then step boldly left and up the overhanging wall to good finishing holds. An exhilarating solo - see the photograph on page 37.

17.   D for Danger HVS 5a * 2010
6m   Start as for the last route but break right by means of the obvious cracks to good finishing holds. A hidden hold in the depths at half height helps - harder for those hindered by bulging forearms!

18. Flakeless E1 5b   2010
5m   The corner until a difficult move left and up can be made. The flake in the name was creaky and was jemmied off before the ascent and can be seen laid out on the ground beneath *Audacity*.

19. Broken Arête MS 4b   2010
4m   Easily up the green arête - poor.

20. Windjammer S 4b   2010
4m   The delightful jamming crack 2m left of *Let's be blunt*.

21. Let's be Blunt S 4a   2010
6m   The blunt arête directly.

22. The Hole Thing VS 5a   2010
4m   Starting from the grassy ledge steeply past the hole.

23. Wind and Piss HVS 5a   2010
7m   The wall and arête to attain a standing position on sloping holds at about 5m, becoming easier above.

24. Hidden Wall 4c   2010
5m   Round the side of the buttress either the centre of the wall, or, just right of the arête.

25. Private Parade 5b 2010
5m Direct up the right side of the wall. Alternatively start on the left at the same grade.

26. Easy 4a 2010
5m The right arête.

27. Eccles Cake Wall VS 5b 2010
5m Climb small ledges past three holes and then left of the flake.

28. Footloose VS 5b 2010
5m The left side of the wall

29. Green Corner 4b 2010
5m Better than it looks.

30. Fruit Slice Wall HVS 5b 2010
5m Fingery strenuous climbing just left of the overhanging blunt rib to good finishing holds.

31. Footless HVS 5b 2010
5m The overhanging steep wall, the difficult move is attaining the last break before the top.

32. The Niche 4c 2010
5m Gain the crack at the back of the niche awkwardly and then use it to gain the top.

The edge then becomes quite broken. Some 700m right are the next worthwhile group of climbs. Walk along the top of the crag until an arête can be seen with a huge thread at mid-height. Walk past this for some 50m to a descent route down the side of rocks (20 fence posts from the main corner post), and then carefully down steep grass before following a narrow path moving back to the pinnacle. The next routes start some 50m north of the pinnacle on the 13m high steep shattered wall.

Photo 5.1: Paul Durkin, **Audacity**, VS 5a * first ascent

33. Almost HVS 5b   2010
13m   The cracks to the niche and up (crux) to reach the terrace. Don't stop here - step right and finish up the wide crack (Given VS in OTM).

34. Nearly HVS 5b   2010
12m   The crack line to two thirds height before a difficult move right to gain the finishing cracks.

35. Just About VS 5a 2010
12m The broken crack line curving right to join the next route.

36. Only Just HVS 5b 2010
11m Step off the sharp boulder to surmount the bulge and reach two breaks. Gibber up from the break to gain the top - surprisingly strenuous.

37. Gotcha HVS 5b * 2010
10m The steep jamming crack with a problematic start. Once established, place your Friends and go! Harder for large hands.

38. Less Fir Tree Wall E1 5b * 2010
6m The steep wall just right of the arête where a long reach is an advantage

39. Little Fir Tree Wall VS 4b 2010
8m The promising looking wall right of the previous route to a good ledge (by a little fir tree!), then scramble up loose rock. Unfortunately promises didn't amount to much here - disappointing!

Before the pinnacle there is much to develop on the intervening buttresses but loose rocks, blocks and flakes need the application of a crowbar and cleaning first. Some cleaning was done and four routes were developed here which are:

40. S Climb E1 5b 2010
10m The crack forming the right edge of the jammed block from a ledge at 2m. Continue leftward to pockets before moving up and right with difficulty to finish.

41. Death by Diamonds and Pearls E1 5c 2010
10m The strenuous crack right of the gravity-defying block at half height. The final overhanging headwall gives interest.

42. The Middle of the Blur E1 5b 2010
10m The arête direct to reach the ledge, climb the wall and the final crack behind

43. That Crack Up There! HVS 5a 2010
9m The cracks forming the V to reach the tricky top cracks.

In the overhanging headwall 20m to the right is a thin finger width crack which has been aid climbed previously using wooden wedges, the remains of which were removed when cleaning. An old peg is also still in place just before the top - a challenge still waiting to be climbed by someone with strong thin fingers.

Right again is the pinnacle, up which gives:

44.   Crack and Block VS 4c   2010
9m   A two pitch route! The cracks to the pinnacle, belay on small wires. Pitch 2, descend to the saddle and finish up the twin cracks.

45. Flaky Pastry S 4b 2010
6m   Start 10m left of Thread arête next to the pinnacle. The RH cracks to the ledge, then up the right hand wall to finish - loose.

The sloping arête to the right invites an ascent - good luck with the top!

46. Did I Offend Someone? HVS 5b 2010
8m   The crack left of *Thread Arête* where a telescopic reach gains a sandy break next to the thread (crux). Finish up the flake.

47. Thread Arête VS 4c * 1958
8m   The crack right of the arête moving to the left of the arête above the huge thread and finishing up the flake.

48. White Flakes VS 5a 2010
8m   Gain a standing position on the flaky white ledge. Straight up the wall on small edges avoiding any temptation to use the crack to the right.

The next two climbs could be considered as just one line, but have been split for completeness.

49. Variety Crack HS 4c 2010
7m   The corner and the wide crack above without the upper corner.

50.   Crack'n'Corner HS 4b   2010
7m   The obvious corner without the upper crack.
51.   Hole in the Wall HS 4c   1958
6m   The right side of the slab, taking care with loose blocks at the top.

Some 10m to the right is a steep slabby wall on which lie:

52.   Very Flaky VS 4b   2010
9m   Start below the obvious flake and climb it.
53.   Powdered Penguin E1 5a *   2009
10m   The centre of the clean wall using small crimps and edges.

54.   Not For T'Short E1 5b *   2010
6m   The arête and small holds on the face - jug finish. Excellent.
55.   Pocket Wall VD   2010
6m   The corner to the ledge, step right using pockets above, short but good.
56.   Pet Project HVD   2010
10m   The series of blocks from the low point using the arête and corner.

Photo 5.2: Simon Royston **Not For T'Short**, E1 5b * first ascent

From the top of the descent to Thread Arête, walk along the top path 125m to the stile. Continue for a further 40m to a diagonal descent route to another buttress 60m along which offers the following:

57.   Central   VS 4c   2013
5m   Climb the middle of the left side of the arête.
58.   We're Jammin'   HVS 5b   2013
5m   Just right, a painful jam to reach the arête, continuing with difficulty
59.   Rowan Wall   VS 4c   2013
6m   Start 4m right on a grassy ledge. Climb the middle of the wall with interest

Scramble along the bottom of the crag for another 60m to reach

60.   The Stretch   E1 5b   2013
5m   Difficulties start from the first step up. Climb the wall to reach the thin horizontal break - well protected with micro wires and/or tiny cams. Step left and stretch up for a good hold before the finishing ledge.
61.   Summer at Last?   HVS 5a   2013
10m   The bottom crack, harder than it looks, to the ledge. Step left and climb the easier shallow corner.

62.   Three Thousand Pounds! VS 5a   2013
10m   The blunt arête just right to the ledge, continue up the arête above.

The next climbs are best reached along the top path - after 75m there's a small buttress, with a rowan tree in front to locate it, on which there are two routes.

63.   Rowan's Shade S 4a 2013
5m   The left side of the buttress either straight up or stepping left to the arête.

64.   Penumbra S 4a   2013
5m   The right side of the buttress.

First Ascents

The edge has been climbed on for many years, but first ascents have not been recorded other than two on UKClimbing.com - one of which, Thread Arête, unfortunately for the claimant had already been done in 1958. This and one other climb at the southern end of the edge near the pinnacle were climbed by Gray West and Malcolm Baxter in 1958, but of other routes little is known or remembered by Baxter. The Black and Tans and The Alpha Club amongst others are thought to have explored the edge in the 1950s, but there is no record of their efforts. A few of the first ascents identified below may therefore be open to dispute. The amount of vegetation and loose rock removed from most of the routes would indicate that they'd probably not been climbed before. Further information on lines, who climbed what and when, and grades are welcome.

1958	**Thread Arête** Gray West, Malcolm Baxter
	Hole in the Wall Malcolm Baxter, Gray West
2009 Oct	**Powdered Penguin** Daniel Lane, Dan Fawley
2010 June	**Broken Arête, Let's Be Blunt, Private Parade** Simon Royston solo
	Hidden Wall Paul Durkin solo
	Easy Malc Baxter solo
	The Hole Thing Paul Durkin, Malc Baxter and Simon Royston
	Crack'n'Corner Matt Rhodes, Malc Baxter and Paul Durkin
	Little Fir Tree Wall Simon Royston, Malc Baxter, Paul Durkin
	Less Fir Tree Wall, Variety Crack Simon Royston, Malc Baxter
2010 July	**D for Danger, Wind and Piss, White Flakes** Paul Durkin, Malc Baxter and Simon Royston
	Eccles Cake Wall Simon Royston, Malc Baxter and Paul Durkin
	Windjammer, Audacity, Green Corner, The Niche Paul Durkin solo
	Fruit Slice Wall, Footless Paul Durkin, Malc Baxter - top roped
	Pet Project Malc Baxter, Paul Durkin, Simon Royston

2010 Aug	**Not For T'Short** Simon Royston, Paul Durkin, Malc Baxter
	Only Just Paul Durkin, Malc Baxter
	Gotcha Paul Durkin, Simon Royston, Malc Baxter
	Pocket Wall Malc Baxter, Paul Durkin, Simon Royston
	Did I Offend Someone? Nick Corbett, Matt Rhodes, Malc Baxter
	Flaky Pastry Matt Rhodes, Nick Corbett
	Almost, Nearly Paul Durkin, Simon Royston, Malc Baxter
	Crack and Block Paul Durkin, Malc Baxter and Simon Royston
	That Crack Up There! Simon Royston, Paul Durkin, Malc Baxter
	S Climb Paul Durkin, Malc Baxter
	Just About Paul Durkin, Malc Baxter, Iain Johnson and Simon Royston
	Very Flaky Simon Royston, Paul Durkin, Malc Baxter and Iain Johnson
2010 Sept	**Death by Diamonds and Pearls** Iain Johnson, Malc Baxter and Simon Royston
	The Middle of the Blur Iain Johnson, Malc Baxter and Simon Royston
	Footloose Simon Royston, Paul Durkin, Malc Baxter
	Flakeless Top roped: Paul Durkin, Malc Baxter and Simon Royston
2013 April	**The Stretch** Paul Durkin, Malc Baxter. Second ascent immediately after by Simon Royston.
	Summer at Last?, Central Paul Durkin, Simon Royston, Malc Baxter
	Three Thousand Pounds!, Rowan Wall Simon Royston, Paul Durkin, Malc Baxter
	We're Jammin' Simon Royston (top rope)
2013 May	**Rowan's Shade, Penumbra** Simon Royston, Paul Durkin

Bouldering Routes: June 2010 **Routes 1 to 15** Paul Durkin, Malc Baxter and Simon Royston, though most of these bouldering routes are likely to have been done by others previously without being recorded.

6 Cowbury Dale

Paul Durkin
OS ref. SD 996014   alt: 300m

The quarry sits above Carrbrook near Stalybridge. The rock is steep, almost vertical throughout, and generally very quick drying though with some seepage from cracks immediately after rain. Belays are sometimes well back on the boundary fence posts of the adjacent Buckton Quarry, the upper perimeter of which is just beyond to the north.

Conditions and aspect: The quarry is generally south facing, with great views out across the valley of Carrbrook and over a wild expanse of moorland to Featherbed Moss in the east. **Routes and bouldering**: 48 routes from Diff to E2. **Parking and approach**: From the B6175 Huddersfield Road, take Buckton Vale Road and go 0.5mile (0.75km) passing a mini-roundabout and then turn left into Carr Rise. Park next to the bowling green. Walk up the road passing the gable end of Beaconsfield Terrace, turn right behind the terrace to the gate signed Cowbury Dale where the quarry track starts. Keep left when the track forks half way up.

Access: The quarry is on CRoW access land with no issues, though peregrines have been known to nest here and barn owls have been seen roosting. Time to the quarry from Carr Rise is 15 minutes.

Descent from the top of the quarry is to either side. For routes finishing below the top of the quarry, descent can be made by traversing heathery ledges to the quarry edges. Take care not to knock stones down when moving away from the top of the routes and beware of tripping over rusty old fence wire hidden in the heather above the right side of the quarry!

The climbs are described from left to right (west to east).

The Far Left Wall

1. Cracked Slab Diff   2008
7m   Up the cracks in the centre of the slab, moving left to finish; the large block in the middle is loose, but going nowhere. Belay a few metres above. Scramble off left below the remnants of the Upper Tier.

2. Surprise HS 4c   2015
7m   Easily up the initial step and wall to what appears to be another easy wall. It isn't! Stay on the left side of the wall. Descend as for *Cracked Slab*.

3. Cracked Corner Diff   2008
8m   Start at the low point and follow the cracks right of the corner. Belay a few metres above, scramble off left.

4. Sidewinder VS 4c *   2008
6m   A nicely exposed one-mover - start 3m up and right of *Cracked Corner*, move up left to reach it and place a runner, before a mantelshelf onto a ledge. Make a cautious balance move up to gain holds on the top before stepping right to finish on the arête. Belay above then scramble off left as previous routes.

The Left Wall

Just right of the grassy corner in the left angle of the quarry, a prominent crack line supports a jammed block.

5.   Footless Pigeon S 4a   2008
15m   Climb the crack using the jammed block then move right at the top to reach the belay ledge of *Crowless Foot*.

6.   Crowless Foot VS 4b   2008
15m   From the back of the V-recess, ascend the left wall of the hanging groove until forced out left at the roof. Easier rock and a short scramble lead to the belay.

7.   Auntie Christine's Bran Cake E1 5b   2015
15m   Start at the centre of the narrow pillar. Head for the left arête by a hard move and keep on it to the top.

8.   Deadleg Crack HS 4b   2008
15m   Move up to a projecting block then gain and climb the steep crack on jams, bridging right into the parallel corner before pulling nicely out left at the overhang to finish on a clean pillar. Belay just above, then scramble up and left to the top.

9.   Super Trooper E1 5b   2008
15m   A full mind and body experience! Climb the left wall to the roof then grunt up the crack with some help from the left arête. Using holds above the final roof, step up right then climb the thin pillar above to reach the top. Continue for 10 metres to a belay at the Upper Tier. Scramble off left.

10.   Rank and Vile HVS 5a   2014
7m   The corner 3m right of *Super Trooper* - an awkward start gains a standing position on the half height ledge. Move up the corner with interest. A traditional HVS!

Six metres right is a crack just left of an arête, which gives

11. The Snark HVS 5a   2008

7m   A short, sharp shock! Jam the crack into and out of the slot. Belay about 2m back at the large block - scramble off right.

12. The Sundog VS 5a   2015

8m   Climb the steep slab directly to the top. Belay as for *The Snark*.

13. Foxglove HS 4b   2015

8m   From the same start, go up the cracks on the right.

14. On Site HVS 5b *   2008

15m   Place side runners in *Sneaky*, then either start directly or, more cunningly, enter from the left to climb the arête (a mini L'Horla... allegedly).

15. Sneaky V Diff   2008

15m   Delightful bridging and jamming up the corner to a ledge where the crack widens at an overhang. Pull onto the left arête and climb it to the heather ledge and belay. The crack can be followed throughout, but less pleasant and not much harder.

16.   Proper Clean VS 5a   2014
10m   An eliminate up the wall right of *Sneaky*. Start 1m right of *Sneaky* heading up and slightly right to a cam placement before fingery moves to the ledge. Scramble up to the belay and escape right. A scrappy finish to the left of the large arête above is possible but hardly worth the effort.

17.   Monster Mantels MVS 4b   2009
10m   At the foot of a crease in the base of the arête reach high holds and a strenuous pull to the ledge before repeating the process to the next ledge. Finish as for *Proper Clean*.

The Upper Tier

A lot of this section right of Monster Mantels *as far as* Call of the Wild, *just left of the final arête, is loose with a bad top. The first explorers dismissed this area, but in 2014 enthusiasts (some may say madmen) cleaned some sections of the top and cleared loose blocks to give the following lines.*

18.   Chorley or Eccles E1 5b   2014
11m   Start below a small corner below the arête before moving to the arête. Move up this boldly without using the loose wall left of the arête. RPs at half height, with a hand placed peg high on the wall after making yet more bold moves. Good finishing holds.

19.   Crossover E1 5b   2014
11m   Start below a wide jagged crack, climb up and left to a foot ledge. Traverse left to the arête to join the previous route. Move up this boldly (peg as for *Chorley or Eccles*).

20. Reservoir Dog VS 5a   2014
10m Follow *Crossover* to the foot ledge before moving back right to the foot of the wide crack. Climb this until a move up and left enables the bottom of a groove to be reached and a final tricky move.
The crack and left edge of the next block was cleaned but not climbed - the bottom half of the crack section looked like it could fall away if stressed by a fall onto a runner.

21. Surfeit of Cakes HVS 5a   2014
10m From the low point of the next buttress climb the crack to a ledge at 5m, making committing moves up the wall to a tricky finish.

22. Wedding Anniversary VS 4c   2014
8m Start just left of the remains of a shot hole at ground level, following the crack line. Finish left of the remains of the upper part of the shot hole.

23. Christmas Butterfly VS 5a   2014
9m The wall to reach the large ledge at 4m left of the overhanging arête. Step right and go around the arête to gain the ledge in the groove. Continue up by a tricky move to another ledge before the final wall.
Gaining the ledge in the groove directly remains a challenge.

Upper Tier Right Side
The following route climbs the right side of the upper tier, starting at the top right corner of the boulder slope from a gap behind a pinnacle which forms the left edge of the Right Wall.

24. Call of the Wild VS 4b *   2008
15m Steep crack climbing with unexpected and nice moves out onto the right arête to finish. Bridge up between the pinnacle and crag to gain the

cracks, then 4m below the top pull right into a sentry box in the right crack. Move immediately right again out onto the right arête, which is followed to the top in fine position. Belay just behind or at the fence.

The Right Wall

The left edge is defined by a green and repulsive-looking hanging crack, which forms the pinnacle on its left where Call of the Wild *starts.*

25.   Green Fang VS 4c *   2008

25m   The crack line gives surprisingly good climbing, not at all as expected; the upper wall, which takes a direct finish to *Call of the Wild* maintains the variety and interest.

1. 10m 4c Gain a position on the right wall before bridging the wide hanging crack until it narrows. Continue to the top of the pinnacle. Now either continue up pitch 2 to the top of the cliff (see below), or belay on the top of the pinnacle, or, with a sling round the top, descend to belay in the gap below. This point can also be reached by scrambling up boulders to the left as for *Call of the Wild*.

2. 15m 4c As for *Call of the Wild*, bridge up between the pinnacle and crag to gain the cracks but having reached holds in the sentry box avoid pulling out right onto the tempting arête and instead regain the left crack and follow it to the top. Belay as *Call of the Wild*.

Alternative start: It is possible to gain the left arête from the left and enter the corner at half height: a nice bold sequence, but it rather misses the point of climbing the crack.

26.   Burning Daylight VS 4c   2008

25m   An exercise in jamming - cams used throughout. Pull steeply out right to enter the crack, then follow it, moving left to a parallel crack and pull over onto the heather ledge with belays above. Move up into the corner on the left until it's possible to gain the left arête and finish as *Call of the Wild*.

The unmistakable and impressive **Chequerboard Wall***, which is criss-crossed by cracks, is down to the right. The first climb on this wall, though initially contrived (rising ground on the left is accessible after 5 metres) gives varied and interesting climbing with a well-protected crux at the top.*

27.   Mein Kampf HVS 5b *   2008

15m   Start from a bramble-covered boulder 2m right of the corner. Twin cracks lead to a ledge. Move left and balance left up steps under the roof. Pull nicely up and out right onto the wall above where increasingly fingery moves follow thin cracks to the belay ledge.

28.　No Need for a Struggle　VS 4c　　　　　　　　　　2009

15m　Start as for *Mein Kampf*, but from the ledge slant right up the crack through bulges to a basin, before stepping out left below a nose, behind which a finger crack leads nicely to the finish and belays of *Mein Kampf*.

29.　Swastika　HVS 5b　　　　　　　　　　　　　　　2009

15m　Hard initial pulls enable the small overhang to be passed before powering up and right to enter a left leaning recessed crack which leads to a basin and possible belay, or the finish of the previous route to the end of *Mein Kampf*.

30.　No Time for New Tricks　E2 5c *　　　　　　　　　2009

15m　Gain a small pedestal at the base of the wall then follow the thin crack line up the face, initially moving slightly left then continuing directly up to a ledge, above which a high slot enables the sloping top to be reached, easily overcome with the help of the crack on the right. Good belay above.

The next route follows the enticing crack line up the centre of Chequerboard Wall.

31.　No Country for Old Men　E2 5c **　　　　　　　　2008

15m　Once up the initial steps, the crack commences with a difficult sequence and continues up sustained and steep rock to the belay ledge. Scramble up and right to reach the top.

32.　Hurricane　E2 5c *　　　　　　　　　　　　　　2008

15m　Climb directly until steep, fingery and difficult to protect moves lead to a step right at 3/4 height to access the final moves of *Jihad* up the top two squares of the chequerboard.

Right, a series of leaning cracks start from a ledge 2m left of the right edge.

33.　Jihad　E1 5b *　　　　　　　　　　　　　　　　2008

15m　Unrelentingly steep and fingery, but worth the effort. Use the short arête to gain the crack and follow it to the overlap where difficult moves left cross two 'squares' and lead up to an inverted-V and exit.

5m right of the corner to the right of Jihad, *a steep buttress stands above heather terraces, with thin cracks in its centre.*

34. Bête Blanche E2 5c * 2014
9m Take easy ledges to the left end of a short wall below an arête. Gain the shelf at 3m, step right to an easy move up the arête to a small ledge which leads to more challenging ones. Use seemingly inadequate holds to step up (crux) and right on small holds (a bit more crux) and then yet more small (but positive) holds until the top!

35. Bête Noire HVS 5a * 2009
8m Short but delightful and well protected technical climbing. Follow the cracks until tricky moves allow access to a ledge before heading up left for a surprise finish. Belay about 7m up the slope.

Right again, three parallel corners will be seen starting half way up the cliff, left of a conspicuous thin overhang at the top of the crag (actually a projecting detached slab of rock). The first corner is 5m right of Bête Noire *and can be gained by scrambling up heather covered ledges or, better, via the start of* Fun in the Sun.

36. Freeborn Man VS 4c 2008
16m An easy start leads to steeper more challenging terrain. Climb the stepped corner to the ledge with the willow sapling and move left into the

steep corner. Pass the first bulge awkwardly, then layback and bridge to a tricky finish. Belay on the large block behind.

An alternative finish at the same grade can be made from the mid-point ledge of the upper section. Step up and left above the bulging wall to reach the top. Traverse left with moves requiring balance to the finish (2015).

37. Fun in the Sun HS 4b *   2008
16m The stepped corner below the arête, starting 2m left of *Mental Mantels* and passing a small ash to gain a ledge on the left, with a willow sapling below an arête. Climb the crack on the left directly, with help from the arête below the top. Belays on either side of the large block on the left.

38. Bridge Too Far E1 5b   2015
16m Follow the lower arête just right of *Fun in the Sun* to a mantel onto the ledge. Move right to the corner and follow it by some tricky bridging and thin protection. A good wire near the top encourages the final (no less tricky) moves. Good belays on either side of the large block 4m back.

39. Mental Mantels E1 5a *   2008
16m A good line on clean rock, with a committing move to gain the halfway ledge - good practice for a similar but harder and more committing move at the top! Follow the lower arête as for *Bridge Too Far*. Move right to the corner, step up and round the arête then climb it with increasing difficulty and minimal pro (small wire) making a final bold mantel onto the top. Belay as for *Bridge Too Far*.

40. Six Steps to Heaven MVS 4b   2008
16m Follow a vague arête, climbing the six large steps to reach a ledge. Go right, into the corner and climb its right wall using parallel cracks to a tricky exit. Belay as *Bridge Too far* or go up and right for fence post belays.

41. The Summertime Blues VS 4b   2008
13m Follow the narrow groove up the wall keeping left of the hanging blocks in the main corner, which is joined not far from the top. Interesting climbing but some creaking flakes. Belay 10m back on fence posts.

The Far Right Wall

A dangerous looking hanging block guards the corner at the start of this west facing wall, which has a nice collection of routes. The first is the yellow corner that descends steeply from overhangs 2m right of the corner.

42. Crusader VS 4c *   2008
13m Climb the corner crack over bulges to the roof, then step boldly out left onto the adjacent prow and stride back right to finish on the hanging arête above the corner. Belay 10m back on fence posts.

43. Jouster VS 4b   2008
13m Follow the cracks steeply to the ledge then bridge up the cracked corner above, moving right on heather handholds to reach the finishing ledges and small tree of the next route. Continue carefully to the top and the fence post belays.

44. Peveril the Poisoner VS 4c   2008
15m Follow the crack system to the ledge and continue up the jamming crack to the small tree. Continue carefully over the heather to belay 10m back on fence posts.

45. Ummayyad HVS 5a*   2008
15m Good steep crack climbing, slightly harder than *Saladin*, and a nice slab to finish.
1. 9m 5a. Slant very slightly left up the cracked wall to a foot-niche at 4m,

then break out left and up to a short thin crack via some nice sequences, gaining the ledge by an awkward move. Belay in the upper crack of the previous route, or continue in a single pitch.

2. 6m 4c. Climb bulges up the centre of the steep slab right of the previous route, and avoiding the edges, before reaching left to the rowan and continuing carefully to the top.

46. Saladin VS 5a *   2008
15m Another good steep crack. Slant very slightly left up the cracked wall as for *Ummayyad*, but continue up before moving up into a niche left of the tower and right of the big ledge. Leave the niche immediately by pulling out right onto the upper wall to finish left of the arête. Belay on the summit block, or on the fence 15m further back.

*The final bold arête of the quarry had been claimed as led after top roping at E4 6b** (but **not** by Tony Howard's team, who did most of the early routes in the quarry). Some expressed doubt that it had been climbed and called it 'The Fool in the Jester Pants'. In 2015 the arête was inspected, cleaned and then climbed. The very loose blocks that were removed and the resultant grade, E2, would seem to indicate that perhaps the previous claim was more imagination than reality. The route is however now very real - worth visiting the quarry if only for this route which is:*

47. Bradley's Hour E2 6a *   2015
15m Take the pleasant 4c initial crack to the large ledge. Gain the small ledge 1.5m higher before stepping down and left onto the front to your last significant foothold. Use the arête, small side holds and some sketchy footholds to reach the ledge below and left of the top - a cam in a pocket and micro wires give some comfort.

48. Twilight Quickstep E1 5c   2014
15m The right side of the arête, starting as for the previous route to the ledge. Thin moves up the wall using the left arête give excellent climbing.

****

First Ascents
(Some routes had been previously climbed by D Cronshaw, Les Ainsworth, Malc Baxter and friends, but were not recorded at the time).

22 June 2008	**Call of the Wild**	A Howard, M Shaw
3 July 2008	**Sneaky, Six Steps to Heaven**	A Howard, D Taylor
7 July 2008	**Crowless Foot**	M Shaw, A Howard
12 July 2008	**Footless Pigeon**	A Howard, M Shaw, S Troop
	Super Trooper	S Troop, A Howard, M Shaw
	Deadleg Crack	M Shaw, S Troop, A Howard

19 July 2008	**Mental Mantels** S Troop, A Howard, M Shaw, W Evans
21 July 2008	**Fun in the Sun** A Howard, D Taylor
	Cracked Corner A. Howard & D. Taylor
22 July 2008	**Green Fang** M Shaw, A Howard
29 July 2008	**Saladin** M Shaw, A Howard
3 Aug 2008	**Peveril the Poisoner** A Howard, M Shaw, D Taylor, M Khano
	Crusader M Shaw, A Howard, D Taylor, M Khano
13 Aug 2008	**Summertime Blues** A Howard, M Shaw
15 Aug 2008	**Burning Daylight** A Howard, M Shaw
23 Aug 2008	**Jihad, Freeborn Man** M Shaw, A Howard, D Taylor
1 Sept 2008	**Cracked Slab, Sidewinder** A Howard, D Taylor
6 Sept 2008	**The Snark** M Shaw, A Howard, S Troop
13 Sept 2008	**The Sundog** A Howard, D Taylor
	This original line ascended what is now Foxglove for 2m before bridging across to the slab and groove. A direct start was added in June 2015.
14 Sept 2008	**No Country for Old Men** S Troop, M Shaw, A Howard
	Mein Kampf M Shaw, S Troop, A Howard
20 Sept 2008	**Hurricane** W Evans, S Troop, M Shaw
Oct 2008	**On Site** C Perrin, R Gibbon
28 Dec 2008	**Jouster** A Howard, M Shaw
29 Dec 2008	**Ummayad** M Shaw, A Howard
27 Jun 2009	**Bête Noire** M Shaw, A Howard
4 Jul 2009	**No Need for a Struggle** A Howard, M Shaw
	No Time for New Tricks S Troop, M Shaw, A Howard
5 Jul 2009	**Swastika** M Shaw, A Howard
11 Jul 2009	**Monster Mantels** A Howard, M Shaw, S Troop
23 Aug 2009	**Green Fang** (alt. start) A Howard, M Shaw
	Sadly this quarry was overlooked in 'Over The Moors' guide. Following this, Baxter, Royston and Durkin took the opportunity to explore and, with help from the original team's script, added a further 17 routes:
5 Oct 2014	**Proper Clean, Rank and Vile** Paul Durkin, Simon Royston, Malc Baxter
	Surfeit of Cakes Simon Royston, Paul Durkin, Malc Baxter
12 Oct 2014	**Twilight Quickstep** Malc Baxter, Simon Royston, Paul Durkin

19 Oct 2014	**Bête Blanche** Paul Durkin, Simon Royston, Malc Baxter
	Sneaked in on a windy showery day when we thought that cleaning was the only choice. Small wires placed for the crux were supplemented by a hand placed narrow blade peg in a hard to spot slot above the small finger pocket.
	Substantial use of crowbars the following week demolished the large tower that stood left of *Surfeit of Cakes*, and revealed *Reservoir Dog* and subsequently *Crossover*.
1 Nov 2014	**Reservoir Dog** Paul Durkin, Malc Baxter
	Named for the perception that each time we visited the quarry, there was a dog swimming in the reservoir.
9 Nov 2014	**Chorley or Eccles** Simon Royston, Paul Durkin, Malc Baxter
29 Nov 2014	**Wedding Anniversary** Simon Royston, Paul Durkin, Malc Baxter
	Sacrifices were made as the sun was out! 17 years for Simon & Lois that day.
	Crossover, Christmas Butterfly Paul Durkin, Simon Royston, Malc Baxter
25 May 2015	**Auntie Christine's Bran Cake** Simon Royston, Paul Durkin, Malc Baxter
	Bridge Too Far Paul Durkin, Simon Royston, Malc Baxter
7 June 2015	**Surprise** Paul Durkin, Simon Royston
	Bradley's Hour Simon Royston, Paul Durkin, Malc Baxter
	The arête was Baxter's project, and he was determined to either check the claimed grade or climb it for the first time. Cleaning revealed extensive loose flakes and accumulated debris, which suggested that a previous ascent was mostly imaginary. Baxter, unfortunately, didn't have the arm span for the crux moves, so success in the end fell to Royston, who at 6' 4" didn't have an issue. It was named for Bradley Wiggin's record-breaking cycling efforts that day.
27 June 2015	**The Sundog** Paul Durkin, Malc Baxter
	After cleaning and removing suspect flakes and a block, the previous dogleg start was straightened to provide a direct start and line, though at a lower grade.
27 June 2015	**Foxglove** Malc Baxter, Paul Durkin
11 July 2015	**Freeborn Man** alternative finish Paul Durkin, Simon Royston, Malc Baxter

7 Cown Edge Rocks and Altar Quarry

By Paul Durkin
OS ref SK019920   alt: 400m

The edge comprises several buttresses strung out along the edge for about 2 miles. The rock is good gritstone varying in height from 3m to 6m. Part way along is Altar Quarry which has some good routes and is higher at 10m. A pleasant day's climbing can be had on the edge or in the quarry. Despite the graffiti, do not be put off by comments in *Over The Moors*.

Conditions and aspect: The initial 60m of the edge faces due east at its north end and east-south-east at No. 3 Buttress and beyond. **Routes and bouldering:** 37 bouldering problems on the edge and 16 routes in the quarry. **Parking and approach:** As for Coombes Rocks to the layby. Then take either of two approaches. First option - walk back up the hill and then down the road to the steep public footpath on the right. About 100m up the path take the stile on the left from where the first buttress is visible. Second option - go through the gate as for Coombes Rocks and then veer left up the hill to reach the top of the edge. Ten minutes from car to edge. Altar quarry is 5 minutes further south. **Access:** The edge and quarry are part of a farm and private property but no difficulties were experienced during work for this guide book. Buttresses are described right to left as approached from the footpath.

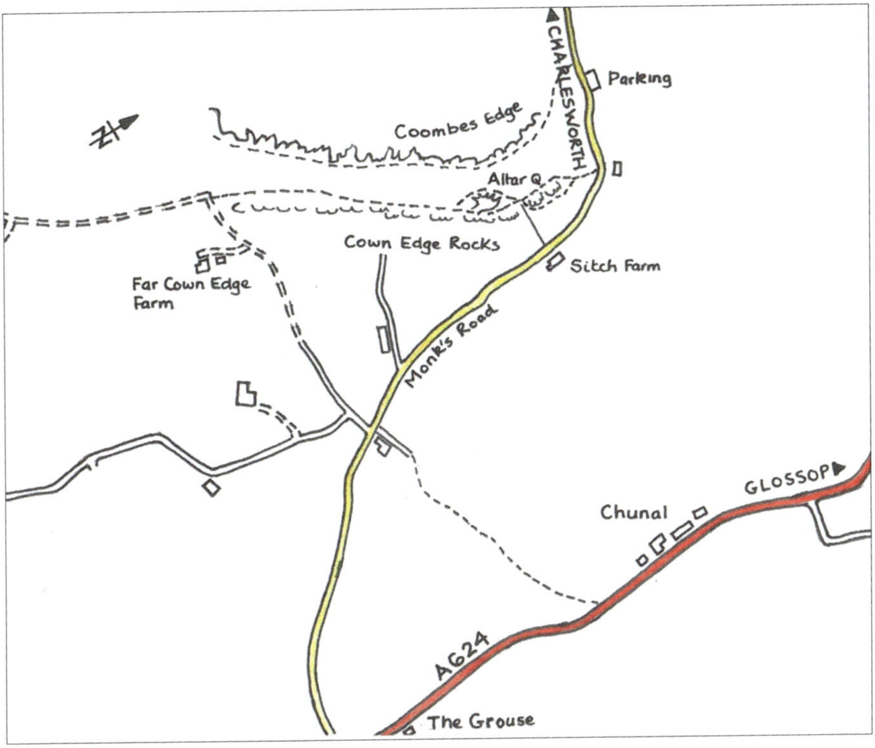

Map 7.1: Cown Edge Rocks and Altar Quarry

Shelf Buttress

No. 3 Buttress Left Wall

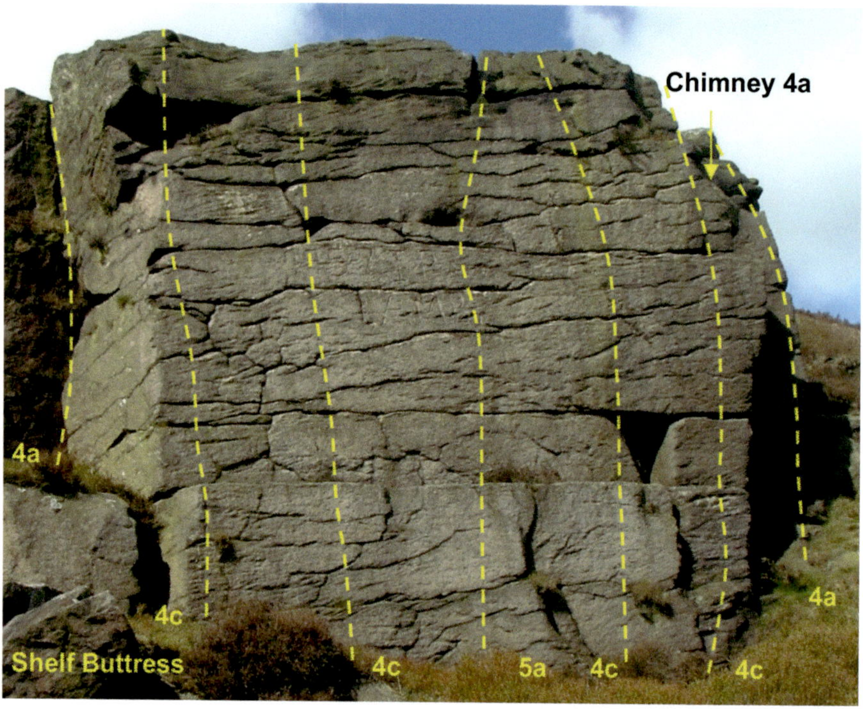
Chimney 4a
4a
4c
Shelf Buttress
4c
5a
4c
4c
4a

4b
4c
4c
4c
4c
4c
5a
4a
Diff
4b
No. 2 Buttress

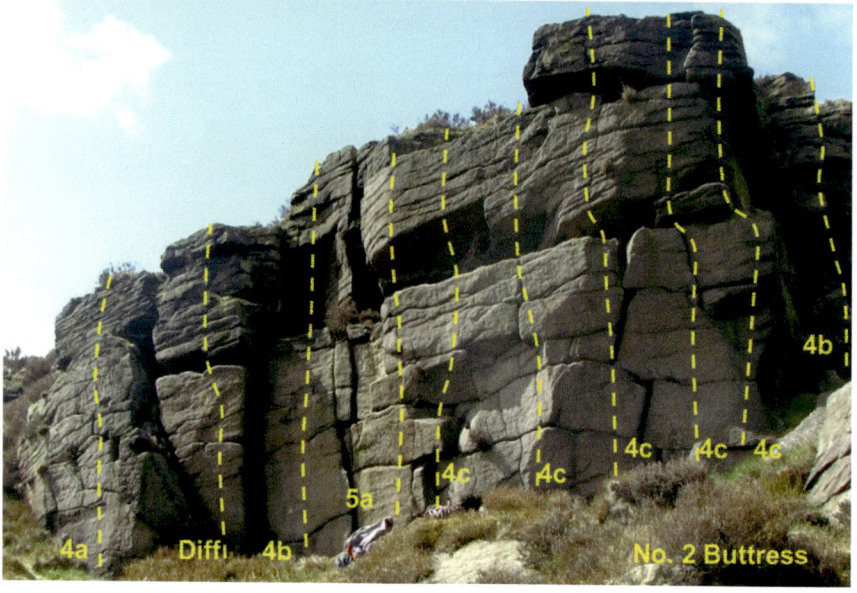

No. 3 Buttress Right Wall

No. 3 Buttress Left Wall

Altar Quarry

The tops and climbs have been extensively cleaned but there may still be some loose rocks that have been loosened by the weather - please take care. Three steel stakes have been placed for belays. The quarry has been defaced by graffiti, but do not let this detract from the climbing.

1.   Busky Buttress S   2012
5m   Enjoy the front of the buttress by whatever's in reach.

*Immediately to the left of the next route, Adri's Arête, is a short wall which can be ascended at 6a - **Surgeon's Stitch-Up** - exceedingly harder if you're less than 1.85m/6ft 1in. tall.*

2.   Adri's Arête 5a   2012
4m   A short problem directly up the right arête of the graffiti strewn wall.

3.   Paul's Wall 5b   2012
8m   The crack and wall through the white chevron and easy wall above.

4.   Altar Crack HS 4b   2011
10m   The altar ledge from the left side, up the carved figures followed by the front of the hanging arête above.

5.   Crackers HVS 5c   2012
5m   The steep crack until an awkward move left to gain the left arête. Finish at the break or continue up the easy top groove of *Beast*.

6.   Beast HVS 5b   1958
10m   For traditionalists! Layback as quick as you like to the loose chock stone and ledge. Breathe again and then take the easy groove above.

7.   Messenger's Destination E2 6a   2014
9m   Takes the left side of the arête. Gain the break using the unfeasibly small crimp in the middle of the wall, the arête and some sketchy pockets. Take the easier wall above through the overhang.

8. Cross Talk HVS 5b 2012
11m Gain the ledge left of the painted cross and circle. Crimp left and up to reach ledges, the sharp left arête and a long stretch to the middle ledge. Continue up the steep wall above just right of the arête.

9. Straight Talk VS 4c 2012
9m The crack right of the circle/cross, to the ledge, from which aim for the top by means of two slots in the upper wall. Beware loose rock.

A worthwhile route can be taken by combining the first part of Straight Talk *with the upper part of* Cross Talk *using an airy hand traverse to give the excellent* **Two Up, One Across** *VS 5a *. The open corner is still available!*

10. Simon's Step VS 5b 2012
9m The corner is harder than it looks.

11. Gosh Josh E1 6a 2014
9m A little artificial but excellent climbing - avoid both the crack on the left and the right arête. Make a hard move to stand on the first ledge before teetering right to take the flake up the wall. Take the easy upper wall.

12. Pillar HS 4c 2012
9m Gain the top of the pedestal and then the easier wall above.

13. Deceptive LH VS 5a 2012
5m Gain the lower ledge before small edges and either an awkward jam or awkward layback lead to better finishing holds.

14. Deceptive RH VS 5a 2012
5m Small edges and cracks - harder than it looks.

15. Yellow Peril 5b 2012
4m Move left and then up using a small slot in the wall and pockets for feet until the ramp can be reached - mantel this to reach the top.

A slightly harder variation though still at 5b is **L Climb** which takes the wall immediately right of the left arête.

****

First Ascents

1958	**Beast** Malcolm Baxter
May 2012	**Busky Buttress** Simon Royston solo
	Simon's Step, Pillar Simon Royston, Paul Durkin
	Two Up, One Across Paul Durkin, Simon Royston, Malc Baxter
	Straight Talk Paul Durkin, Simon Royston
	Adri's Arête, Paul's Wall, Cross Talk Paul Durkin solo
July 2012	**Crackers, Deceptive LH, Deceptive RH** Paul Durkin, Adrienn Angyal and Malc Baxter

	Yellow Peril Paul Durkin solo
March 2013	**L Climb** Simon Royston and Paul Durkin solo
March 2014	**Messenger's Destination** Malc Baxter, Paul Durkin, Simon Royston

At 73 years old Malc went up this like a monkey up a tree. This was not true of the seconding team who struggled and whimpered! This had been top roped previously by Adrienn Angyal and Malc Baxter, when Royston and Durkin still couldn't follow!

Gosh Josh! Simon Royston, Paul Durkin both on a top rope, led clean by Royston and Baxter 29 March 2014.

Surgeon's Stitch-Up Simon Royston

****

Re-joining Cown Edge, there are some significant gritstone chunks spread along the edge on which lie:

About 1km further along the edge is a unique buttress characterised by large holes - climb all over it, there's nothing harder than 4c.

Continuing, if you look further west you might spy a triangular shaped buttress a further 1km's walk away - make the effort to get there where the following short problems can be found.

The 5c problem does not use either the arête or the hole - if you're shorter than 1.83m/ 6 foot it'll be harder, if not impossible.

8 Crook Hill

Paul Durkin
OS refs. SK 182871 & 184869   alt. 380m & 370m

These groups of rocks are situated on the north side of Ladybower Reservoir on two hill tops which together form Crook Hill above Crookhill Farm. There are two distinct areas to visit for a rewarding day's bouldering.

Conditions and aspect: Both areas face south west and get the sun and are sheltered from northerly winds. Good gritstone with great views over the reservoir and The Snake Pass. **Bouldering:** The north-west hill top of Crook Hill (first map ref.) has 8 easy lines (4a to 5a). At the south-east hill top of Crook Hill (second map ref.), there are 25 lines (4a to 6c) and at The Slab 75m away, a further six (4b to 5c). Thirty-nine in total. **Parking and approach:** From either direction on the A57 Snake Pass, park in the layby east of the bridge, opposite Ashopton. Walk west and then turn into the Derwent Valley road, cross the road after some 50m and take the path marked to Crookhill Farm. Alternatively, drive approximately 1 km down the Derwent Valley road to the first parking bay on the right. Walk back to the access road to Crookhill Farm, which is followed to a gate just short of the farm where the two alternative routes converge. Follow the path to the north of, and past, the farm until you can see a rock outcrop on the skyline as shown below. For the central area, pass the rocks to the right and turn left beneath them. After 50m the first group of rocks can be seen. For The Slab, continue around the hill for 75m. For the boulder, walk to the outcrop and go left. The hill top to the NW is reached by a path easily visible from the outcrop. The lines are on the SW side. **Access:** No problem.

The problems are described firstly at the NW hill top 200m from the boulder; the hill top of Crook Hill (above); and finally The Slab 75m away.

First Ascents

UK Climbing records one climb **Jonathon Livingstone Steel Fingers** at f7b (trad 6c), as a 6m high slabby wall on crimps, near the hill top. This is the centre of the middle wall mentioned above, but it measures 4.75m not 6m. No doubt the others have been done before but are identified here for the record.

There are also some easy lines on rocks left of those shown above.

Walking back to the SE hill top of Crook Hill, follow the path to the top, above the rocks, where at the high point, a large boulder lies square to the edge. Variations on the middle routes, eliminating some, or all, of the larger hand holds offer some entertainment at 5b.

Below the boulder is a pillar - the front or left side are the same grade.

Move down a little and 30m eastward, the first set of blocks have numerous easy problems. The middle of the central block has been

Crook Hill

climbed at a significantly harder grade. The right side of the arete has been done, but grade unknown. Spotters are advised for the left and central walls as they sit on a terrace above a significant drop.

Below these are some large(ish) boulders which give:

75m south east lies a slab which appears to be blank. However, there are footholds in the lower 1.75m which with the aid of strategic pebbles for your hands (or not as the case may be!) enables the top to be reached.

The left-most line is only 5b if you're 6' 4" or taller - for those smaller it's almost impossible unless you can spring off one foot on a tiny toe hold. The top block can be scaled in a couple of places at 4c.

Paul Durkin on the 5b+ balancing for the foothold only crux on The Slab.

Simon Royston reaching for the Juggy top on a 4c at the NW hill-top.

9 Crow Stones

Paul Durkin
OS ref SK170970   alt. 500m

The edge comprises good quality moorland grit that has probably never been seriously assessed before the work undertaken for this guide - or at least no records have been found. The edge consists of three tiers of buttresses that are generally sound clean course grained gritstone with climbs varying in length from 3m to 8m. The rock enjoys the sun from late morning and is quick to dry out. None of the routes are particularly high in the technical grades but the situation and quality of climbs make it a good day out.

Conditions and aspect: Lots of sun throughout the day. The edge is largely west facing with fantastic views down the Derwent valley to the south and Bleaklow to the west. **Routes and bouldering:** 45 problems from Diff to 6a. The lines are mainly boulder problems but there are several routes for which you may wish to use a rope. **Parking and approach:** Vehicular access is either from the south from the A57 at Ladybower, or from the north from the A628(T) just west of the Flouch roundabout.

From the south (A57) take the turnoff to the Derwent Valley, drive for about 2.5 miles north to the visitor centre at Fairholmes. You then have two alternatives - on Mondays to Fridays continue northwards for another 5 miles to Kings Tree where parking is available at the bus turnaround, or, at weekends park at Fairholmes (or one of the free parking areas before reaching Fairholmes) and catch the 222 bus to King's Tree. The bus service operates on Saturdays and Sundays and is at intervals between 50 and 90 mins from Fairholmes starting at 09:20. A single service originates from Bamford Station at 09:00am - beware, the last bus leaves King's Tree at 17:15pm, returning to the station at 17:45 (Times correct for 2016 - please check for the current timetable).

From King's Tree follow the track northwards past Slippery Stones to the attractive 17th century pack horse bridge, relocated in 1959 from the now flooded valley. Continue northward until you can turn right up the clough between Crow Stones edge and Bull Stones. Follow the track all the way to the skyline at an altitude of 500m, then head north west again towards a group of stones visible on the skyline - you've arrived! An hour and a half from the car park at Kings Tree to the stones.

From the north, park just east of the 'Dog & Partridge' off the A628 at Milton Lodge, taking care not to block the road or any vehicular entrances. Continue on foot down Hordron Road about 1.5 miles taking the right fork heading for a single storey stone building in its own stonewalled courtyard. Skirt around the building continuing on the track down the steep hill to a wooden footbridge in the valley bottom. Take a deep breath and then follow the track southwards steeply up the left side of the clough, past shooting butts and then a further mile until the Crow Stones can be seen on the skyline. Either plough across the moors (hard work!) or take the path left to Outer Edge then turn right to the stones. About 5 miles, 1¾hrs and plenty of sweat. **Access:** The buttresses are in open countryside on CRoW land.

Top Tier

1.	**Beaky** 5a	2009
7m	The front of the left fin.	
2.	**7m** 4b	2009
3.	**7m** 4b	2009
4.	**6m** Diff Anywhere up the front of the angled blocks.	2009
5.	**4m** 5a	2009
6.	**Bulge** 4m 5a	2009
7.	**4m** 4c Right side up the flute	2009
8.	**3m** 4c	2009
9.	**6m** 5a	2009
10.	**6m** 4c	2009

The right side of the arête also gives a 4c line.

11. **6m** 4b Right side of the buttress on slabs right of a crack   2009
12. **3m** 5b   2009

Top Tier - Back and Side

13. **Green Step** 6a   2009
3m Make a hard move on the right side of the arête.
14. **Brown Wall** 3m 4b   2009
15. **7m** 5b   2009
16. **8m** 5b   2009
17. **Pedestal** 5b   2009
8m Gain the pedestal via an overhanging wall. Step up onto the wall to scary moves to the top.

Middle Tier

The middle tier looks inviting but unfortunately is not high enough to provide many problems - two have been done on the left end of the main section. The 'Rocking Stone' at the left end of the tier, while being quite impressive and tempting, is probably totally unsafe.

18.	5a	2009
19.	4c	2009

Lower Tier

The lower tier is a boulderer's delight - over twenty lines have been climbed with undoubtedly room to squeeze some more in. The tier is sheltered from the wind and dries out rapidly. Some 10m in front of route 23 is a steep 3m high slab - the left edge is 4c, the middle 5b.

20.	4m 4a		2009
21.	4m 4b		2009
22.	**Tempter** 5b		2009

4m The wall without using the left arête.

23.	5m 4b		2009
24.	4m 4b		2009
25.	4m Diff		2009
26.	**Hanging Around** 5c		2009

4m Overhanging wall just right of the arête - the critical hold is where?

27.	4m 4a		2009
28.	4m 4a		2009
29.	4m 4a		2009
30.	4m 4a		2009
31.	**Green Fingers** 5a		2009

4m The middle of the green wall

32.	**Teeterer** 5a		2009

4m The top without using either the left arête or right crack line

33.	**Go On!** 5a		2009

4m The right wall of the buttress between the arête and the crack line.

34.	5m 4b		2009
35.	5m 4c		2009

36. Grassy Hole VS 4c   2009
5m Straight up!
37. 5m 4b   2009
38. 5m 4a   2009
39. High Stepper 5a   2009
5m Not as hard as it appears with a bit of thinking!
40. Boulder Trundle 5a   2009
4m The short arête and wall above trending right for a hidden bucket.
41. Trepidation 5a   2013
4m Start just left of the previous route making awkward moves to attain a standing position on the ledge. Easier moves lie above.

The overhang left of Trepidation *was looked at and fallen off with monotonous regularity on the day, with the conclusion that this should be left for others more capable.*

42. 4m 5b   2009
43. 6m 5c   2009
25m left of the lower tier is a 3m high slab - traverse from right to left (without the edges) at **5b**.

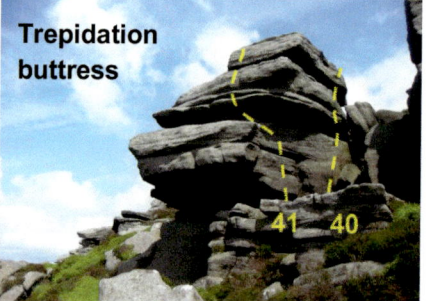

Trepidation buttress

First Ascents

2009, 16 September, 18 to 40, Paul Durkin and Malcolm Baxter, all solo except **Grassy Hole** led by Baxter.

2009, 27 September, 1 to 17, 42, 43, Paul Durkin, Simon Royston, Malc Baxter and Matt Rhodes, all solo.

2013, 21 August, **Trepidation** (no. 41) Paul Durkin, Malc Baxter

The rock needs little in the way of cleaning other than some cursory brushing.

10 Crowden Great Brook, Shield and Easter Buttresses

Paul Durkin
OS ref SK063015   alt. 400m

The 'Over The Moors' guide mentioned these two buttresses in passing but didn't identify where the routes were - read on! The two buttresses are a delight to climb on - prime examples of good moorland grit. The buttresses are sound clean coarse-grained gritstone with climbs varying in length from 5 - 14m. The rock basks in the sun for most of the day and is quick to dry out. None of the routes are particularly difficult but the situation and quality of climbs make it part of a good day out for any climber.

Conditions and aspect: Lots of sun throughout the day. Both crags are west facing with fantastic views of Laddow to the west and Crowden Castles to the north. **Routes and bouldering:** 8 routes from VD to E1. No specific boulder problems - the results of jumping off or a slip could lead to a change in your sport to sky diving into the brook below! Belays at the top of the routes are generally good. **Parking and approach:** Vehicular access is from the A628(T) at Crowden. There's a car park immediately on the left after leaving the A628(T). Follow the Pennine Way for a short distance then the valley bottom staying on the right side of Crowden Great Brook as if heading for Crowden Castles. Where the brook bends to the right below the grotty green River Buttress, continue for a further 200m where Shield Buttress can be seen some 30m up the hillside. Easter Buttress is a further 200m north at approximately the same contour line. 30 - 40 minutes from car park to the first buttress. **Access:** The buttresses are in open countryside on CRoW land.

Shield Buttress

1. Mace VD 2009
6m The left side up to and past the wide crack.

2. Shield VS 4c 2009
7m Over the small roof past the hollow flake which somehow clings on.

3. Cutlass VS 4c 2009
6m Right side of the wall.

Easter Buttress

4. Port Side VD 2009
6m The wrinkled wall and arête on the buttress' left side.

5. Yardarm VS 4c 2009
14m The left side of the buttress. Along the lip to the large ledge to easier ground.

6. Merlin VD 2009
12m Start as for *Yardarm*, and move up the middle of the narrow buttress all the way - a good traditional climb.

7. Lapwing E1 5a 2009
5m Two small roofs taken directly in the middle - catcher strongly advised.

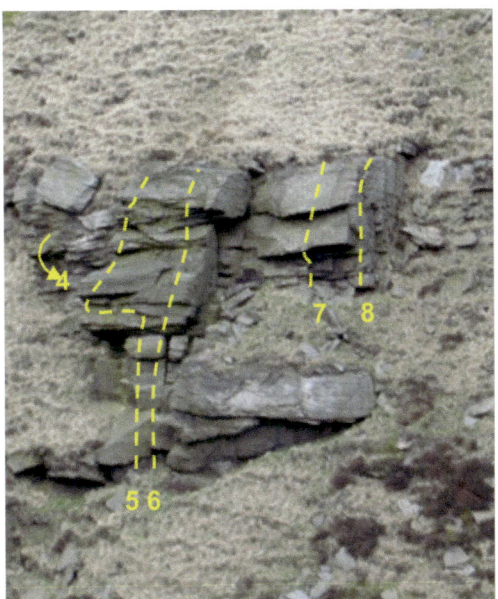

8. Linnet VS 4c 2009
5m The right wall and arête immediately right.

****

First Ascents

2009 April   **Mace** Malc Baxter, Simon Royston, Paul Durkin
                  Shield, Merlin, Linnet Paul Durkin, M Baxter, S Royston
                  Lapwing Paul Durkin solo
                  Cutlass, Yardarm Simon Royston, P Durkin, M Baxter
                  Port Side Simon Royston solo

The rock needed little in the way of cleaning, other than clumps of heather and grass from the tops, with some brushing undertaken as the routes were climbed.

11 Dovestones Boulders

Paul Durkin
OS ref. SE 023026   alt: 310m

The boulders sit below the Dovestones Lower Right Quarry, strewn haphazardly between the stile from the track and the quarry face.

Conditions and aspect: The boulders are generally west facing, with great views out across Dovestones Reservoir and the Chew Valley. **Bouldering**: 35 routes from 4b to 5c. **Parking and approach:** From the A635 'Isle of Skye' road between Greenfield and Holmfirth, about ½ mile from Greenfield take the right turn to Dovestones Reservoir and the Sailing Club. Park below the dam (Pay & Display £1.30 all day in 2017), walk past the sailing club at the south end of the reservoir, then go left following the east side of the reservoir and after approximately 700m take a rough path up right and through a small plantation which brings you out at the Lower Right Dovestones Quarry. Where the track lies below the quarry, cross the stile and scramble across some 20m of broken ground to the first boulder, which is on the right. **Access:** The boulders are on CRoW access land with no issues.

Dovestones boulders from the stile in the fence

Breakfast Boulder

Horned Boulder

Just right is a narrow slab.

Behind this are two further slabs

Just right and down is the Polish boulder - named after all the slots [Zlotys]

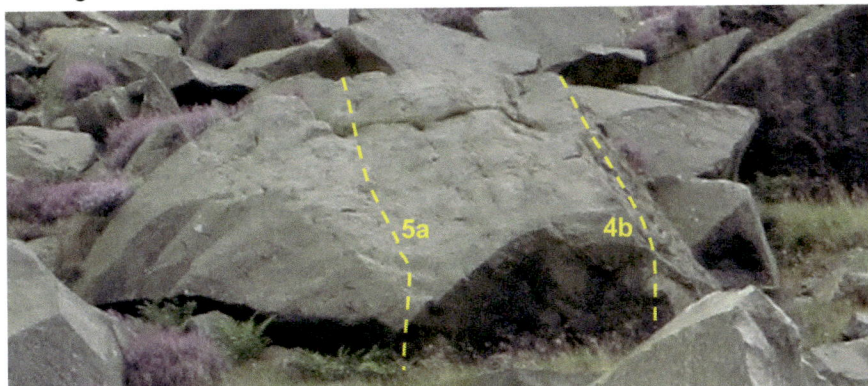

Behind and up from the Horned boulder is the 'Scary boulder'. Named for

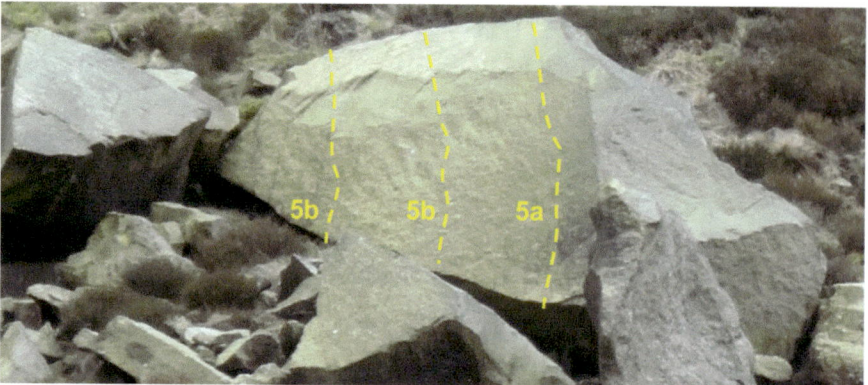

the horrendous landing at the right-hand end - a catcher is needed to brace their legs across the gap - see below.

Malc Baxter on the 5a with Paul Durkin fielding.

Just up the hill are two boulders, the upper with a concave face. Be warned, descending from the top of the boulder needs a cool head.

At the back of the upper boulder is:

Scrambling down t'other side is:

Heading back right again, tucked away in an alcove in front of the Horned Boulder is a mantelshelf and an easy overhang problem:

Left again is another opportunity for yet more steep slab work

Over to the left are some easy problems - an easy arête and an introduction to padding moves on a slab

Directly up the slope is a rough looking boulder with a rowan tree growing behind it. One line currently goes directly up the front.

High up the slope on the left is a slab with a black wall on its left

Traversing left across the hillside to the next group

12 Doctor's Gate Circuit

This provides some of the most enjoyable bouldering, not the hardest, but certainly guaranteed to give satisfaction at the end of the day. The circuit is on good rough moorland gritstone with plenty of sunshine (you hope!) and some of the best wild moorland scenery. For those with an ornithological interest, kestrels are likely to be putting on displays below the crags you're climbing on, particularly Lower Left Shelf Stones, while buzzards ride thermals above the whole circuit and beyond.

Parking and approach: The circuit is a moorland walk of just over 5 miles (8.5km), from The Snake summit to Old Glossop, or vice-versa, visiting 6 bouldering sites in exposed positions which add to the experience. Ideally, get dropped off at The Snake summit, then it's an overall downhill circuit (From Old Glossop it's a much more strenuous route).

At The Snake summit, park on the gravel at the roadside and follow the Devil's Dike (Pennine Way) north for some 1400m before taking a track left heading for the 621m high trig point of Higher Shelf Stones. Before you get there, go left around the shoulder to reach Lower Right Shelf Stones.

From Old Glossop, follow Shepley Street to the turning circle and park near the railings or bushes. This is the start of the Doctor's Gate Bridleway. Follow that straight on to Mossy Lee Farm, cross a bridge and bear left up the hill. At a signpost (near a barn) keep left uphill. Follow the path around the back (east) of Shelf Benches when the James's Thorn boulders can be seen. That path leads to the boulders and crosses the fence at a stile. Alternatively, if you want to go to Near Ashton Clough first, before reaching James's Thorn (before the fence) head to the right across the moor.

Access: There are no access problems at any of the sites as they are in open countryside - and what countryside! There are currently 58 listed boulder problems - less experienced climbers might be advised to take a short rope for some of the higher problems at Lower Left Shelf Stones and Near Ashton Clough.

Details are in the following sections: Lower Right Shelf Stones; Higher Shelf Stones; In Between Shelf Stones; Lower Left Shelf Stones; James's Thorn; and, Near Ashton Clough. The larger crag of Lower Shelf Stones, included within the 'Over The Moors' guidebook, is passed when walking from In Between Shelf Stones and Lower Left Shelf Stones.

Lower Right and Higher Shelf Stones has in particular been visited previously but there are no records (that Baxter could find).

Baxter declared that, although a biased opinion, he considered that this was one of his all-time favourites "cos I could do it from our 'ouse". Climbs have been described assuming you're approaching from The Snake summit.

Doctor's Gate Circuit

Map 12.1: Doctor's Gate Circuit - Location Map

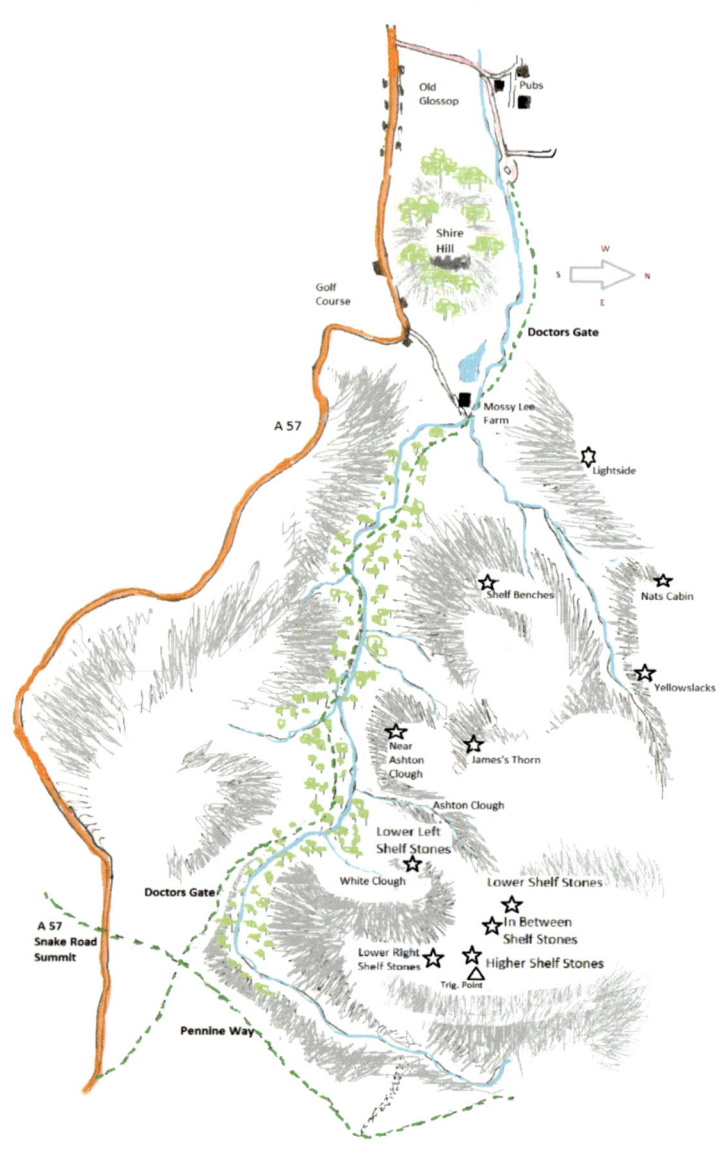

Source: Malcolm Baxter

12.1 Lower Right Shelf Stones

Malc Baxter
OS ref. SK089947   alt. 595m

Approximately 100m south of Higher Shelf Stones - two outcroppings in a great situation - all day sun, and rough moorland gritstone - approaching from the Snake summit this is the first outcrop. **Bouldering:** 12 problems up to 5b, and 4m high. **Parking and approach:** 40 minutes from The Snake or 1 hour 35 minutes from Old Glossop.

1. 4b
2. 4b
3. 4c
4. **Bloodstain** 5b * - Excellent.

5. **Legover** 5a
6. 4a Centre of small buttress on slopers.
7. 4a The blunt arête.
8. **Black Face** 5b * The centre face without arêtes - excellent.
9. **Black & White** 5a * Excellent.

Moving a little further northward to the next two buttresses, the next three routes are on the west side just left around the arête.

10. **The White Face** 5b * No arêtes! Excellent.

11. 4a
12. 4a

All except 7 climbed by Malcolm Baxter during 1960 - 2007. Number 7 was climbed by Paul Durkin during checking in July 2015.

12.2 Higher Shelf Stones
Malcolm Baxter
OS ref: OS089948   alt. 615m

This is a collection of boulders near a popular trig. point with great views some 100m north of the Lower Right Shelf Stones. See the Local History section at the end of this chapter for more information on the air-crash site just to the east. **Bouldering:** Some 14 problems, some wishing to be a bit longer, but generally containing good technical moves. **Parking and**

approach: As for Higher Right Shelf Stones, 45 minutes from The Snake or 1 hour 30 minutes from Old Glossop.

1. 5b The left arête using the last letter 'T' of ELLIOTT.
2. 5a - 2ft right of 1.
3. **Yeabut** 5c Excellent(ly hard).
4. **Nobut** 5c No easier!

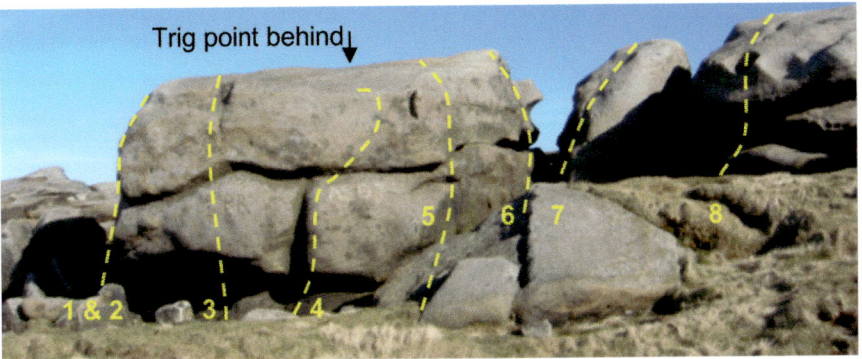

5. **'Eadbut** 4b good
6. 4b At letters 'KA'.
7. 4b
8. 5b Two hole slab full frontal or 4c swing from the right.
9. 5a
10. 5b * Without the LH cleft, 5a with. Good for learning to trust your feet!

11. 5a
12. 5a Sit start to rock over.
13. 4b Avoid the hold on 14.
14. 4c Press using the one hold.

All climbed by Malcolm Baxter between 1960 and 2007 except 12 by Iain Johnson, and the cleft elimination on no. 10 by Paul Durkin in July 2015 during checking. Not forgetting to acknowledge previous, unknown visitors.

12.3 In Between Shelf Stones

Malcolm Baxter
OS ref: SK088948   alt. 590m

An exposed position on the moor edge between Higher and Lower Shelf Stones. **Bouldering:** 2 problems which fit in with the Doctors Gate Circuit, possible scope for more. **Parking and Approach:** 50 minutes from The Snake or 1 hour 25 minutes from Old Glossop.

1. 5a
2. 5a Through the pocket, which involves some pain for the fingers.

Both climbed by Malcolm Baxter, 8 February 2008.

12.4 Lower Left Shelf Stones

Malcolm Baxter

OS ref: SK084946   alt. 520m

This small crag is on a spur running down to the south of Lower Shelf Stones. **Conditions and aspect**: Some brittle rock but a superb, isolated, and sunny position. **Bouldering**: 9 lines of modest grade up to 5b. **Parking and approach**: As above but if approached from Old Glossop continue to James's Thorn and follow the top fence past the remains of a plane crash continuing straight ahead when the fence heads right, 1hr 15 minutes, or 50 minutes from The Snake.

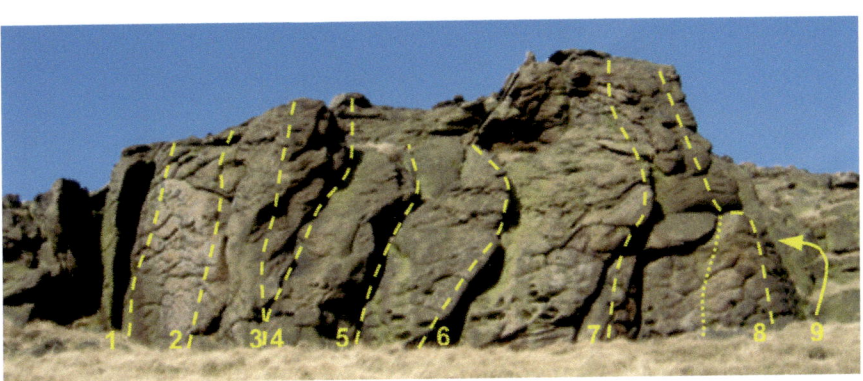

1. 5b The wall to an interesting finish.
2. 5a The steep crack.
3. 5a The front of the steep wall.
4. 4b Layback the flake.
5. 4a The wide crack.
6. 4a Another layback.
7. 4c Steeply pleasant.
8. 4c The blunt arête for 2m, step left and ascend the upper section just left of the arête. The direct start is slightly harder.
9. 5a * Takes the wrinkled end wall direct, aiming to reach the arête at about two thirds' height.

Most of these climbs were checked by Malcolm Baxter and Jack Christian in 2008, with 3 more added (1, 3 and 9) by Paul Durkin in September 2015.

12.5 James's Thorn
Malcolm Baxter
OS ref: SK 078948 alt. 520m

Lots of boulders, some delivering more than would be expected. **Conditions and Aspect**: The boulders face southwest in an open situation near the top of Shelf Moor, and get lots of sunshine. They are easily incorporated with a visit to other Doctor's Gate sites. **Bouldering**: There are 13 listed with limited scope for others. **Parking and Approach**: Nearer Old Glossop rather than The Snake, but is still a pleasant outing from there.

1. 4c The wall.
2. 4b/4c The jamming crack.
3. 5a The wall 1m right of the corner. 4b the easy corner.
4. 4b You want it to carry on after gaining the front.
5. 5a But feels a bit harder.
6. 5b * Competent footwork needed for the wall and then to overcome the classic slopey top.
7. 4b Right arête.
8. 4b Slab, step left up the 4c arête. Alternatively go up the crease just right at 4b.

9. 5a/b * The steep wall just right (looks easy!).
10. 4a Easy crack.
11. 5b Directly up the nose of the buttress.
12. A 4c pull over the top, which needs thought.
13. So does this one, also 4c.

12.6 Near Ashton Clough

Malcolm Baxter

OS ref. SK079943   alt. 400m

Conditions and aspect: Three small isolated outcrops of excellent quality and great situation overlooking Doctor's Gate and Shelf Brook. Very sunny, best suited to people who enjoy a good walk on the moors with boots and a chalk bag in their sack. Part of the Doctor's Gate circuit. **Bouldering**: 8 problems, most less than 6m. **Parking and approach**: Park at either The Snake summit and follow The Pennine Way north before heading left via Higher Shelf Stones, or park at Old Glossop and follow the Doctor's Gate path before turning left uphill heading for James's Thorn boulders, but before reaching them (before the fence) head to the right across the moor, 55 minutes. There are alternative approaches.

This buttress is the left-hand of the three - 100m left of the centre buttress

1. **Black Fingers Wall** 5b - good.

2. The flake and left sloping fault 4a.

The centre buttress is a quality piece of rock with excellent problems.

3. **Doctor's Delight** 5b * arête on its left - excellent and satisfying.
4. **Cure-All** 4c
5. **Brain Strain** 5c/6a * depending on your height and the condition of the holds.
6. The right arête 4a, or, near the top, traversing left to the centre of the wall is slightly harder.

The right-hand buttress is approximately 100m rightwards and higher, on which lie.

7. A delightful Diff.
8. 5b * With easier variations.

All climbed by Malcolm Baxter during 1990 - 2007.

Local History

This is one of the highest parts of Bleaklow, and there've been several air crashes, the most notable being at Higher Shelf Stones and James's Thorn.

At James's Thorn, Lancaster Mk.X KB993 No.408 Squadron RCAF crashed on 18th May 1945. The aircraft was flying from RAF Linton-on-Ouse and had earlier been carrying out bumps and circuits, but the crew became tired of this and decided to fly around the local area. As it became dark the crew became disorientated and eventually ended up circling Glossop. The aircraft was observed flying into the hillside at 10:10pm. There is a memorial to the crew of the aircraft on James's Thorn. The demise of KB993 was one of the first post-World War 2 crashes on high ground, ten days after the end of hostilities. The memorial for KB993 also commemorates the crew and passengers of C-47 Dakota 42-108982 which crashed nearby on July 24th 1945.

At the top of Bleaklow, scattered far and wide throughout a large gully system east of Higher Shelf Stones, can be found the remains of *Overexposed*, an American World War Two-era Boeing RB29 44-61999 Superfortress bomber (the RB29 was the reconnaissance version of the B29). The plane came down on 3rd November 1948, but over 68 years on, many major structural spars remain, undercarriage struts, pulley wheels for internal control cables, and even large sections of the light aluminium alloy from which the fuselage was constructed, have survived the ravishes of the Bleaklow weather. The most instantly recognisable parts of the aeroplane are the 18-cylinder Wright R-3350-23 engines, still in a remarkable state of preservation. The theory is that she was flown into the ground by instrument malfunction and/or pilot error, and it is obvious from the state of the wreckage that the crew wouldn't have stood a cat in hell's chance of surviving the impact.

13 Photographs

This is where we take full advantage of being the authors - we choose them! Biased towards our own, we've (really) tried to include others.

Photo 13.1: Malcolm Baxter, **Sniffle,** first ascent E1 5b *, Marsden Clough

Source: Paul Durkin

Photo 13.2: Malcolm Baxter, **Bloodstain**, 5b *, Lower Right Shelf Stones

Source: Paul Durkin

Photo 13.3: Simon Troop, **No Country for Old Men**, E2 5c, Cowbury Dale

Source: Tony Howard

Photo 13.4: Adrienn Angyal, **Two Up, One Across** VS 5a*, Altar Quarry

Source: Malcolm Baxter

Photo 13.5: Simon Royston, first ascent **Oroxylum Indicum**, E1 6a

Source: Malcolm Baxter

14 Ironbower Rocks

Malcolm Baxter
OS ref. SK 117997   alt. 380m

Conditions and aspect: Facing south-west it gets the sun all day. Small weathered moor edge buttresses conveniently situated near the road. Some traffic noise depending on wind direction. Generally sound but some gritty holds. **Routes and bouldering:** More than 45 problems which have all been soloed. The average height is less than 5m with grades from 3b to 5b. **Parking and approach:** Opposite the crag is a track which leaves the A628T road and goes down to the Woodhead Tunnels where there is ample parking. Walking back up the track and across the road, it is necessary to negotiate a fence which keeps the sheep off the road. However, a better alternative is to follow the Pennine Trail up left from the parking area, cross the road and continue onto the moor where it is necessary to negotiate a new length of fence, and follow the moor edge south-east to the rocks.

1.   3b
2.   An improbable step right to easy ground 4c
3.   A project - something left for climbers in the future!
4.   Right side of the arête 5a
5.   Small arête with help from the left 4c

6. Pleasantly at 3b.
7. Pull over small overhang 3a
8. Left edge 4b
9. Centre 4c
10. Right again without the arête 4a
11. The projecting flake 4b
12. Easy buttress VD
13. Left to right VD
14. Excellent wall 5a
15. Arête 5a
16. **Mop Up** Leaning arête 4a
17. **Ripoff** Steep thin crack and arête 5a good, strenuous
18. **Brevity** VD
19. **The Nose** Direct from the right 4c
20. **Off-Hand** Overhang via short crack 5b
21. **Right-Hand** The RHS of the niche 4b
22. **Clutch** 5b Quality, 5c for the short
23. **Clamp** 5b Quality, 5c for the short
24. **Cornerstone** HVD
25. **Dignity** 5b Good
26. **Gravity** 5b Good

27. **Topology** HVS 5a Good, but you may feel the need for a rope!

28. 4b
29. 5b (5a for the tall)
30. Arête on left side 4b, on right side it's Diff
31. 4a
32. 4c
33. 4c
34. Crack 4c
35. 5b A good dyno, harder for the short

36. 4b
37. Diff.

38. 4a
39. 4a
40. 4b
41. Right again through the wide crack at high level 4b
42. Just left of the next route 5a
43. Rounded bulging arête 4c
44. Rounded twisting arête 4b alternative start on the left at 5a
45. Front of the arête 4c
46. Anywhere on the slab 4b
47. Hanging arête - another left for future climbers - very challenging.

****

First Ascents

The majority were done by Malc Baxter and others over many years and compiled / checked in 2007/08. Some, like the fine arête of Topology, must have been done before, though no details were found. A further 10 routes were found during checking by Simon Royston and Paul Durkin in 2009.

15 Longdendale Trail Rocks

Malcolm Baxter and Paul Durkin
OS ref. SK042976   alt. 180m

Good climbing mainly on slabs. Usually damp in winter, but gets the afternoon summer sun. Don't be put off by the green, the rock is good quality - if it were at Stanage, climbers would be all over it like a rash.

Conditions and aspect: Brilliant for cyclists with boots and chalk bag, not much more of an effort if you're on shanks' pony. **Routes and bouldering:** 38 climbs have been soloed from Moderate to 5b and there's scope for more. **Parking and approach:** The rocks are next to the Longdendale Trail which has many access points and parking at Hadfield and Torside. There is a barbed wire fence along the bottom of the crag, but a wooden section at the south west end near route 1 provides safer access. Please note that the Trail is owned and managed by United Utilities and you may be asked to leave - there is no agreement in place for climbers.

1. Right arête 4c
2. Centre 4c

3. Right arête 5a
4. The pod-like crack and slab 5b *
5. The winding crack 4c *
6. Block and wall behind 5a (LH finish 5b)
7. Right of centre to grassy ledge 5a

8. Left of the arête 5b *
9. From a shelf with a small oak tree, the right side of the slab 5a
10. The centre trending slightly right 4c
11. The left side 4c
12. Right arête 4c
13. Centre - pleasant V.Diff
14. Left - pleasant V.Diff
15. Up and right to reach the arête 4c
16. Up the centre over the overlap. Excellent 5a
17. Left of centre up the black streak 4c
18. The leftwards leaning arête Moderate
19. The crack in the slab avoiding the arête 4b
20. The slab between the crack and the arête avoiding both 4c
21. Right arête not using holds on the central route 5a *
22. Central. Excellent 5a *
23. Left of centre 5a *
24. The slab, slightly harder if the pockets are avoided 4b

25. The steep wall and the one above that 4c
26 The sharp flake and slab above 4c
27. The centre straight up past a slot 4c, or,
28. A steep start just left to a recess then right to the previous climb at a similar grade

A little further left is a lonely slab
29. Centre of the slab 4b

Some 30m left is a small 4m high wall, split by a crack at its left side, which provides a surprising number of problems over its short length.

30. The right arête 4c
31. The centre of the wall between the thin crack and arête 4c
32. The thin crack direct 4c
33. The centre of the wall left of the thin crack 4c
34. The wall just right of the wider crack without using the crack 5a

The wider crack can be climbed but is scrappy.

35. The wall L of the wider crack through the scoop 4b
36. Start a bit lower and left of the previous route - the blunt arête 4b

Some 10m left is another wall with a cherry tree in front of it.

37   Start from behind a cherry tree, ascend the block and then climb the wall just left of the arête without using it! 5a

38   Start as the previous route but go leftwards from the block 4c

****

First Ascents

2007 Sept 1   Ten climbs by Malcolm Baxter and Paul Durkin, all solo.

2009 July 25   A further seven, numbered 4, 6, 8, 9, 11, 21 & 22 added by Paul Durkin, Malcolm Baxter and Simon Royston, all solo.

2009 Aug 2   Another nine, 30 to 38 added by Paul Durkin, Malcolm Baxter and Simon Royston, all solo.

2014 Apr 27   A further 12 added by Paul Durkin, Malcolm Baxter and Simon Royston, all solo.

16 Long Gutter Edge

Malcolm Baxter
OS ref. SK070976   alt. 390m.

A collection of small buttresses which have heather growing up to the rocks and very suitable for beginners and people who like solitude or to solo.
Conditions and aspect: Good rock which dries quickly and a sunny west aspect. **Bouldering:** 12 climbs from Moderate to HVS 5a. The first 5m are best but some can be extended to 10m. **Parking and approach:** Park at Torside Pay & Display, cross the Longdendale Trail, follow a path which eventually turns right towards Torside Clough, continue until necessary to break steeply up left to the crag. Time: 30mins. **Access:** No problem.

1. The isolated rib Moderate and very pleasant.
2. Rib with undercut start VD
3. Wall left of central crack HVD
4. The central crack VD
5. Centre of blank wall right of crack VS Good
6. Short slabs followed by a short vertical section HS
7. Undercut slab with a flake crack on its left HS
8. Slab with undercut break VS
9. Steep wall by pockets VS Very Good
10. Just right of 9. Left side of arête and thin crack HVS 5a *.
11. Right side of arête Severe
12. Rib with tricky move HVS 5a

Climbs 1 - 11 Malc Baxter 23 June 2003, 12 Simon Royston 6 July 2003

17 Middle Black Clough

Paul Durkin
OS ref SK115988   alt. 450m

A great day out for those who like good moorland grit with a view. Comprising six buttresses stretching some 60m characterised by rounded breaks and tops and steep faces, varying from 4 to 9m. As a bonus there are three boulders further up the valley which offer good problems for a bit more walking. For the truly adventurous there is the scariest 4c problem located 250m west of these boulders on the Near Black Clough east bank.

Conditions and aspect: The edge faces just south of east and gets the morning sun with most buttresses getting some in the afternoon. **Routes and bouldering**: 17 routes from S to E1 on the main edge and 10 recorded problems at the boulders. **Parking and approach**: A track leaves the A628(T) on its south side and descends to the Woodhead Tunnels - parking after 150m on the left. A very pleasant (and challenging) walk follows. Cross the juvenile Etherow River and over the stile on the left heading east. At the junction with the stream emanating on the right from Black Clough follow the stream on its right to a level area just past the point where the track doubles back up the hillside. From here the challenge starts - 30m past the flat area, cross the stream and follow it until after 10 mins you reach a 10m high waterfall. Continue on its left for a further 15 mins until the edge can be seen around the bend high on the right. Continue until 30m past the southern end of the edge - cross the stream at a tree, climb straight up to a 2m high boulder, skirt this to the right and head up to a more substantial boulder with a 'porthole', head diagonally right to the crag. 40 minutes from car to edge. **Access**: The edge is on open moorland with no access restrictions.

Main Edge

Routes 2 and 3 may need a brush after winter as they tend to grow lichen. Worth the effort in cleaning as they are some of the best on the crag.

1. Yeti VS 4b — 2009
6m The left side of the lower wall to the exposed upper rounded section.

2. Pure Green E1 5b * — 2009
8m The centre of the lower wall to gain the left end of the block, the steep wall above on thin holds.

3. Brown(ian) Motion HVS 5a * — 2009
9m The wall's right side - gain a stance on the block and then the wall above. Better protection than it looks.

4. Literate VS 4c — 2009
4m The middle of the wall.

5. Litter Arête E1 5b — 2009
5m The awkward rounded arête.

6. Dyslexic VS 5b — 2009
5m The middle of the wall avoiding the right arête.

7. Surety S 4b — 2009
5m The pleasant arête starting at the lowest left end point of the front wall, moving to the left side after 2m.

8. Uncertain HVS 5a — 2009
4m The wall to the right side and above the cave to an exciting heather grabbing top.

9. Jagged Edge VS 5a — 2009
4m The arête and parallel sharp crack steeply to a good finish.

10. Jammer HVS 5b — 2009
4m The overhanging crack with a gymnastic start - the upper crack can be hard on the hands.

11. Judge Jeffreys HS 4b — 2009
3m The hanging arête starting from the left.

12. Rope VS 4b — 2009
4m The steep wall 2m right of Judge Jeffreys.

13. Pierrepoint VS 4c — 2009
4m The middle of the wall.

14. Furry Crack S 4b — 2009
5m The steep crack direct.

15.   Skinned VS 5a *   2009
4m   Furry Crack to the good jug, move right on good holds to the blunt arête and exposed top - a good (h)airy route.

16.   Oak Quest HVS 5a   2009
6m   Initially the blunt arête, move right and the wall above to a thin top.

17.   Where's That Oak Gone! HVS 5b   2008
5m   The right side of the buttress to finish as for Oak Quest.

Paul Durkin, **Brown(ian) Motion**   Malc Baxter, **Furry Crack**
(Both photographs taken on first ascents)

Boulders

Three boulders that are worth a visit, grouped on the east side of Middle Black Clough and visible on the skyline some 150m south of the main edge. The problems are:
1.   4c, Climb diagonally left to a tricky finish.
2.   4c, Left side of the arête.
3.   4b, The wall 2m left of the arête.
4.   5b, Right side of the arête to a stance and then easily to the top.
5.   5a, From the lowest part of the boulder, straight up.
6.   4c, Achieve a standing position on the left end of the boulder.
7.   5a, Start at a small crease directly below the blunt arête - climb it.

8. 5a, Do the same thing 1m right.
9. 5a, Start as for either of the last two routes, traverse right on the lip for 2m before heading up.

The Scariest E2 4c. This sits half way down the east bank of Near Black Clough, 500m north west of the boulders, seemingly defying gravity, which must surely win in the end!

Descend the 45° slope, go left of the boulder (looking down) to a small stance. Trying not to picture the horrendous fall below, gain a standing position and then pad to the top.

Malc Baxter, first ascent of *The Scariest*

First Ascents
Main Edge
2008 Oct	**Where's That Oak Gone!** Malc Baxter, Paul Durkin and Simon Royston
2009 April	**Brown(ian) Motion, Skinned, Oak Quest** Paul Durkin, Malc Baxter
	Yeti, Furry Crack Malc Baxter, Paul Durkin
	Dyslexic, Pierrepoint, Uncertain, Jagged Arête Paul Durkin solo
	Litter Arête Paul Durkin, Malc Baxter and Simon Royston
	Literate Simon Royston solo
	Judge Jeffreys, Surety Malc Baxter solo
2009 Oct	**Jammer** Paul Durkin solo
	Pure Green Paul Durkin, Malc Baxter
	Rope Malc Baxter solo

Boulders
2006 Jan	**4, 7** Malc Baxter
2008 Nov	**1, 2, 3, 5, 6, 8, 9** Paul Durkin
2008 Nov	**The Scariest** Malc Baxter, Simon Royston

18 Mount Famine

Malcolm Baxter
OS ref. SK055849   Alt. 410m

A small outcrop, high above Dimpus Clough, which has one of the finest situations in the district with extensive panoramic views of Kinder Downfall and the surrounding countryside.

Conditions and aspect: Morning sun. North faces can be green but most rock is good and clean. **Routes and bouldering:** One quality route with the rest (24) having been soloed as problems. Scope for eliminates. Average height is 5m or less. **Parking and approach:** Drive from Hayfield towards Chapel-en-le-Frith and at the top of the hill turn right into a lane and park on the left opposite Peep-o-Day Farm. Walk 100m back towards Hayfield, cross the road and take a farm track signposted Public Bridleway just before a house. At a T junction of tracks turn right and follow the track to the hollow between Mount Famine and South Head (after two gates), and follow a path left up the shoulder to the rocks. Or, more direct and interesting, at the T junction go forward through a gate signposted Footpath and Bridleway, and after two more gates follow footpaths right to a steep ascent to the rocks. **Access:** No problems.

1.   Jiggly 4b
Wall and crack.

2. Wiggly 5a
Recessed corner to join Jiggly
3. Figgly 4c
Awkward crack with old ring peg and something else wedged in
4. Moderate up the scooped recess
5. Frog's Mouth 4c
Scale the overhung roof
6. Gripply 5a
Right arête passing a beak on its right.

7. Slabs 4a
8. Crack 4a
9. Just right without the crack 5a
10. Left arête, undercut start and sloping shelf 5a
11. Just right, a crack to a sloping shelf 4c
12. Wall just right of the previous route 4c
13. Left wall heading rightwards 5c - top roped
14. **Zeitgeist** E1 5c *   2007
6m Strenuous moves through the overhang and straight up by a crack.

15. A recess 4a
16. 6m right the arête without the crack 4c
17. Immediately right - the wall 5a
18. 2m right is another crack 4b
19. The right arête without the crack 5a
20. Sit start overhang 5b
21. 5m right is the last small buttress - sit start 5b

15m almost directly below is a large boulder. Start 22 and 23 by stepping off a large slab block.

22. **Gill Pot** The left arête 5a
23. **Quart Pot** Step up then down before climbing direct up the centre 5b excellent
24. **Pint Pot** The right arête 5a

About 500m NW near the footpath at SK050855 is a small overhanging buttress with one worthwhile problem, **Lonesome**, through the middle at 5a.

Malc Baxter giving it some on *Lonesome*.

****

First Ascents

2006-2008 All the climbs and problems were developed by Malc Baxter, Simon Royston, Joe (Matthew) Rhodes and Paul Durkin acknowledging that some have been done before, particularly **Figgly** done by Malcolm Baxter in the 1960's and who else? **Lonesome** was added in 2012 with **Frog's Mouth** in 2017 during final checking.

2006 **Gill Pot, Quart Pot** Malc Baxter
     Pint Pot Simon Royston
2007 Sept 8 **Zeitgeist** Malc Baxter, Simon Royston - both solo
2012 **Lonesome** Paul Durkin solo
2017 **Frog's Mouth** Paul Durkin solo

19 The Naze

Malcolm Baxter
OS ref. SK 041835   Alt. approx. 300m

These are part of a group of small outcroppings below Cracken Edge Quarries. This is a quiet and isolated spot - delightful!

Conditions and Aspect: Facing just south of east they get the sun for a lot of the day and the most interesting rocks are just below the brow of the hill and often enjoy a bit more shelter. **Routes and bouldering**: 21 boulder problems with three at 5a and three at 5b, though the rest are generally not very hard. Other buttresses above and nearby give nothing harder than difficult to severe and are not described but give satisfying solos. **Parking and Approach**: At Chinley where the B6062 changes from Green Lane to Buxton Road turn north off the B6062 to cross the railway, turning left to park on Stubbins Lane opposite the war memorial. Turning right after crossing the railway puts you on Maynestone Road - parking is not recommended here because it is narrow. Walk 250m northeast along Maynestone Road and take the first signposted footpath on the left - follow this to the field and head straight to the top of the hill where there's a stile. Don't cross the stile but turn right and keep the fence on your left, and continue to follow the track/path to another stile. Over the stile, immediately bear right and the rocks are below - the best are below a large silver birch which is situated 10m below the crest. Half an hour from the car to the crag.

1. Easy
2. Diff - ignore the protruding nose on the next buttress.

3. 4b The front face in the middle - the left and right sides of the face go at the same grade.
4. 4b The right face of the buttress with an enticing hold up right.
5. V Diff The left arête of the next buttress
6. V Diff Anywhere up the front just left of the highest point
7. 4b Take the wall and crack directly below its highest point
8. 4c Start at the low point avoiding any holds in the scoop / cut out up and left.
9. 4b The crack at the back of the corner using the block for feet. Go left to finish easily on the ledge above.
10. 5a - The rear crack going straight up *without* using the block on the left - if you use this only award yourself 4c. Continue straight up with care to finish.
11. 5a - The overhanging left arête finishing as for the previous route.
12. 5a - The face going right to a mantel. Finish here or continue up the easy crack
13. V Diff - The cracks throughout
14. **Top Pocket** 5b
    6m Make difficult moves up the wall to reach a shallow pocket which at best gives the ledge (or a swift descent!). Continue by finishing up the arête.
15. 4c The wall just right behind the block. Step onto a sloping foothold to ascend the wall without using the block to your rear. Finish straight up left of the tree.
16. 4b The crack to the tree
17. 4c The wall just right - just enough holds keep appearing to complete the route
18. 4b The crack just right.
19. 5b The wall just right without recourse to either of the bounding arêtes. A tad artificial but entertaining.
20. 5b The blunt arête direct using holds no further than 300mm either side of the arête - as the last one - artificial but entertaining.
21. 4a The right arête to the good ledge.

First Ascents
All routes by Malc Baxter and Simon Royston in 2009 except 18, 19 and 20 which were climbed solo by Paul Durkin 4 May 2013.

20 Ogden Clough

Paul Durkin and Malc Baxter
OS refs. SK042972 and SK043971   alt. 280m

Two quarries - one small one next to the road and one big one some 500m uphill. Suitable for bike or walking visits.

Conditions and aspect: *Over The Moors* dismissed the upper quarry as 'the worst quarry in the world, if not the Peak' - sadly it has only been of local interest but deserves more, especially now it's been 'cleaned'. Ignore the green which may be there following periods of wet. **Routes and bouldering:** 10 problems at the Roadside Rocks and 22 routes/problems in the upper quarry. **Parking and approach:** Situated next to the B6105 near the 'Devil's Elbow' approximately 3k from Glossop. There's parking for three cars in a layby some 50m west of the Roadside Rocks, which is 20m back from the road next to a small plantation. If approaching from Glossop it is recommended that you drive past the Devil's Elbow to a farm entrance, turn round and drive back to the layby. The other larger quarry is accessed from a stile in the layby and then up and left along a track going behind the plantation, which after 10 minutes leads to a stile at the quarry entrance. **Access:** Roadside Rocks - situation unknown but no previous problems. The upper quarry is on access land.

Roadside Rocks

The climbs all feel serious because the ground falls away steeply from their starts. Catchers are advised.

1. 4m 5a
2. 4m 5a

Ogden Clough

3. 5m 5c
4. 4m 4b
5. 8m 4c - you may feel the need for a rope!
6. 4m 4c
7. 4m 4c
8. 4m 5a

Right and just up the hill is
9. 4m 4b The left crack
10. 4m 4b. The right one

Upper Quarry

As you come over the stile, directly in front of you is this attractive scooped chunk of rock. When you've done these two problems, done in the 60's, think about the footwear used - no sticky rubber!

11.   4.5m 5c   1960's
Feels scarier than it should.

12.   5m 5a   1960's
Start as for the previous route but go right.

13.   5m 5b   2014
On the right side of the arête is an overhanging wall. Use the arête to assault the wall. At the top, hand traverse right to the easy corner. The enthusiastic gymnast may want to try going over the top - good luck!

As you will have noticed, right of the scoop is a rather large expanse of rock, which as far as the author is aware, has not had any recorded climbs. With lots of cleaning and crowbar work to remove loose rock, 19 routes were unearthed. It's not a quarry for the faint hearted, with most routes having a serious feel to them. Don't be put off though, there are some excellent routes. Be careful in the Wallnut Plug *area as a barn owl uses the upper ledge right of that route as a roost.*

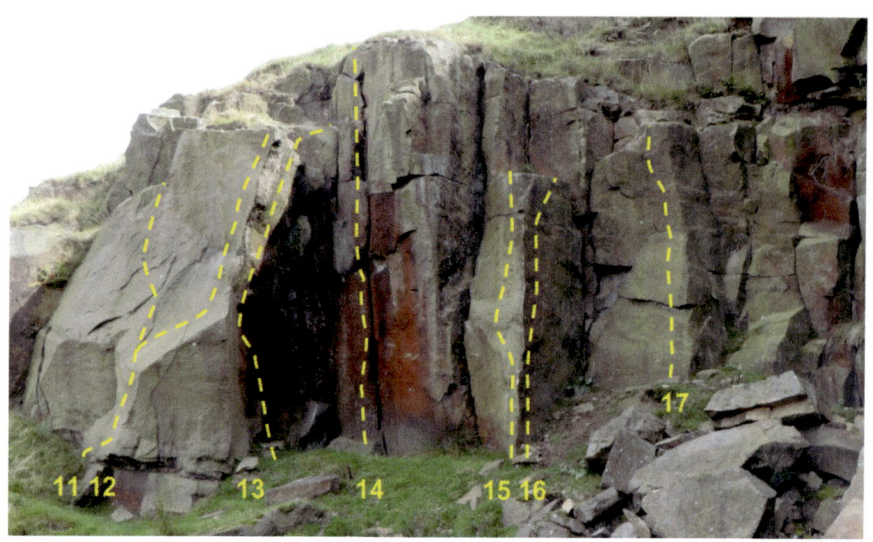

14.	**Redbreast** 6m 4a	2014
15.	4m 4c The arête and wall on its left.	2013
16.	4m 5a The arête on its right before a tricky move to top out.	2013
17.	4m 5a The wall left of the arête - feels quite nervy!	2013
18.	**Guinea Gold** HVS 5a	2013

17m Easy ground to the ledge before climbing the crack on the left side of the arête. Alternatively, the wall right of the arête at the same grade (if you're tall!).

19.   Juggler HVS 5a   2013

20m The series of steps left of the corner to the ledge before assaulting the steep wall (crux) to then continue up blocks and arête on its left.

20.   Cobnut Flake VS 5a   2014

20m Climb the small dirty corner for 4m before moving left to a niche. Climb the leaning blocks on the right to the bottom of an overhanging chimney(ish) crack. Climb it.

21.   Ogden's Nut Gone Flake VS 4c   2013

15m Starting 1m right at a small corner, follow the cracks up the steep wall - better than it looks. Finish at the large ledge.

22.   St. Julien VS 4c   2013

15m Start 1m right of the previous route up a(nother) narrow corner to a ledge before climbing the crack formed by the leaning blocks.

23.   Barling Royal Hunt VS 4c   2013

15m The corner to the ledge and then the cracks just to its right

24. Battle Axe HVS 5b   2013
15m The arête promises a lot but doesn't quite deliver, nevertheless a worthwhile route with good lower and upper sections and well protected. A tricky lower wall to reach the ledge at 5m. Continue up the corner for 5m until you can move onto the front using a pocket. Finish at the upper ledge

25. St. Bruno VS 5a   2014
15m The corner right of Battle axe arête. A scrappy start which gets better with height. The top 5m above the ledge provides the crux.

26. Gold Block HVS 5b   2014
15m Starting 1m left of the large undercut block climb the wall between the two cracks with continuous difficulty to the ledge. Finish easily up the top broken band of rocks.

27. Lanyard VS 5a   2014
15m Immediately left of the undercut block is a wide crack which is followed to a small ledge at 6m. Stay with the wide crack to the crux to reach the larger ledge, stepping up and left to stand on it. Finish as for Gold Block.

28.   Walnut Slice E1 5b   2014
15m This time starting 1m right of the large undercut block, up the cracks to the ledge. Step left to climb the thin crack to the triangular hole, before moving left and up using the arête to reach the upper ledge by some tricky moves. Follow the awkward groove above.

29.   Walnut Plug HVS 5a   2014
15m Start as for the previous route to the ledge, continuing up the cracks to the next ledge and the awkward groove.

30. Robin S 4b   2013

10m The two clean walls 10m right separated by a scramble up easy ledges. Very pleasant.

31. Rough Shag 6a   2014

5m Using just the (painful) central crack (strictly avoiding the left arête and crack line to the right) make an enormous step onto the narrow ledge at chest height, finishing easily above. Do not be tempted to step off the grass just right. Significantly harder for those shorter than 1.93m (6' 4"). Just left, the wall and slab between the arête and central crack gives **Midnight Flake**, a pleasant 5a problem.

****

First Ascents

1958	**5** Malcolm Baxter
1960's	**11, 12** Malcolm Baxter
2003, 2 April	**4, 6, 7, 8** Malcolm Baxter
2013, 11 June	**1, 9, 10** Paul Durkin
2013, 7 July	**Guinea Gold** Simon Royston, Paul Durkin, Malc Baxter

	The Juggler Simon Royston, Malc Baxter, Paul Durkin
	Barling Royal Hunt Malc Baxter, Simon Royston, Paul Durkin
2013, 14 July	**Ogden's Nut Gone Flake, Battle Axe** Paul Durkin, Malc Baxter
2013, 21 July	**St Julien** Paul Durkin, Simon Royston, Malc Baxter

The route hadn't been as vigorously cleaned as normal - at the first try Durkin finished upside down after pulling up using both hands on what appeared to be a solid flake on the topmost block - and was still holding the chunk of rock! After taking a breath, he managed to choose a spot to throw it clear of the otherwise occupied second whilst still upside down.

	Robin Malc Baxter, Simon Royston, Paul Durkin
2014, 7 April	Roadside rocks: **2** Paul Durkin
	3 Simon Royston
2014, 9 Aug	**St Bruno** Malc Baxter, Paul Durkin
2014, 16 Aug	**Walnut Plug** Simon Royston, Paul Durkin, Malc Baxter
2014, 24 Aug	**Cobnut Flake** Malc Baxter, Simon Royston, Paul Durkin
	Gold Block Paul Durkin, Malc Baxter Simon Royston
	Walnut Slice Simon Royston, Paul Durkin, Malc Baxter
2014, 7 Sept	**Lanyard** Paul Durkin, Simon Royston, Malc Baxter
	Midnight Flake Malc Baxter, Simon Royston, Paul Durkin
	Rough Shag Simon Royston

Old Pits

21 Oldpits Quarry Boulder and Edge

Paul Durkin
OS ref. SK 051881   alt: 340m and 390m

"There is a boulder in the middle of the quarry, which has a few problems from 4b to 6a" said the 'Over The Moors' guide for Oldpits Quarry - this chapter builds on the good work of that guide by shedding more light on these problems. Added to this is the product of exploring the collection of small buttresses on the sky line above the quarry.

Conditions and aspects: The boulder sits in an eastern facing quarry with sun from early morning to late afternoon. The view from the quarry is surprisingly good and takes in the whole of Kinder Downfall and the adjacent approach edges. The sky line buttresses are some 50m higher, also face east with the same view and a bit more. **Bouldering**: 5 routes from 4b to 6a on the quarry boulder; 8 routes from 4b to 5c on the sky line.
Parking and approach: From the Bowden Bridge car park east of Hayfield, continue up the road to where it splits after 600m - take the left option through the gate and follow for 300m until a steep cobbled path strikes left up the hill. Follow for 200m to the top before turning back left to follow the level track, thickly overgrown with ferns, for 300m to the quarry. The quarry floor can be on the boggy side so boots are recommended, or wait for a heat wave. Takes about 15 minutes from the car to the boulder.

For the sky line edge, continue past the turn off for the quarry along the cobbled path for another 50m until a track turns off left up the hill. At the gate keep left and follow the path until you reach the track to the hunting lodge and a steel footpath sign. Take the narrow path southwards until you meet a dry-stone wall which is followed until the wall turns westward. The wall is broken down at this point - pass through and you're at the edge buttresses. Takes about 25 minutes from the car to the edge.

For a pleasant day it's recommended that the edge buttresses are visited first. Then, having ticked all the problems, drop straight down the steep hillside keeping left of the fence. This takes you down to the south end of the quarry where the boulder awaits.
Access: The boulder and edge are on CRoW access land with no issues.

Oldpits Quarry Boulder
Because of lack of traffic, it's advisable to take a stiff brush to the holds before putting in the effort - especially the 6a. Line 3 is the easiest descent.

The overhanging north-west face has yet to receive an ascent - good luck!

Edge Buttresses

22 Park Bridge

Paul Durkin
OS ref. SD 943024	alt: 134m

Located near Oldham, the rock is steep, almost vertical throughout, and generally quick drying. The rock could be described as 'could be better', is predictably brittle, and is for those who like a challenge. Belays are available from three steel tubes driven into the top of the crag. When you've found the stakes and thought that they're easy after a top-roped inspection, try leading them!

Conditions and aspect: The quarry is south facing, with good views from the top out across the Rocher Vale. From the east end the remains of the engine house can be seen from where a steam engine pumped water from the nearby Rocher Pit coal mine. **Routes**: 6 routes from VS to E1. **Parking and approach**: From the B6194 Lees New Road, take Alt Hill Lane and go 0.35mile (570m) before turning right onto Alt Hill Road, an unmade suspension challenging road. After a further 0.35mile at the bottom of the hill turn right into Park Bridge where parking for several cars is available. Walk east up the track next to the river for 230m to the quarry.

Access: The quarry is in a public park but the access status is unclear - the checking team experienced threats of legal action - so please assume there is no right to climb. Time to the quarry from the car park is 5 minutes. Descent from the top of the quarry is to the east side by the obvious path down the ridge. The climbs are described from left to right (west to east).

1. **Billet** E1 5a   2015
15m Carefully climb the lower wall below the broken overlap. Ease over this to climb the wall above heading for the ledge below and left of the tree. The wall above is not hard but feels exposed as runners are few.

2. **Bar** HVS 5a   2015
14m Start up the small wall below the crack or, just right at the groove, to the small ledge. Follow the cracks with some difficulty to the ledge. Move 2m right and ascend the short wall.

3. **Centre Buckle** E1 5b   2015
12m Start just right of the oak tree stump (as it was in 2015) directly below a wide slot at 4m. Climb to the slot before tentatively stepping down and left to the crack line which is followed directly to the large peapod and the top. Not for the nervous.

4. **Elastic Modulus** E1 5a   2015
15m Start as for *Cold Steel* until after 3m look fearfully at the leftward slanting crack and follow it to the top. Needs a cool head.

5. **Cold Steel** VS 4c   1961
10m Start 1m left of the arête - head for the broken crack which finishes, strangely enough, 1m left of the arête.

6. **Equal Angle** VS 4c   2015
9m From the base of the tree move onto the arête - climb to better holds and the top!

****

First Ascents
Cold Steel had been previously climbed solo by Malc Baxter in 1961 but was not recorded at the time other than in an old black and white photograph. Although we could find no proof, most of these routes have most probably been top-roped before we got there.

1961	**Cold Steel** M Baxter (solo)	
	The original route soloed by Baxter may have started a little further left, but finished in the same place.	
6 June 2013	**Billet** S Royston, M Baxter	
22 Mar 2015	**Elastic Modulus** S Royston, P Durkin, M Baxter	
29 Mar 2015	**Bar** M Baxter, S Royston	
19 April 2015	**Centre Buckle** P Durkin, S Royston	
26 April 2015	**Equal Angle** S Royston, P Durkin, M Baxter	

23 Swan Clough Quarry
Paul Durkin
OS ref SK119994   alt. 300m

Conditions and aspect: The climbs are on parts of a quarry thought to have been used for the adjacent water company's assets and dry-stone walling. The quarry comprises three walls, two facing North and the middle one West. The routes are few and not particularly high but are well worth a visit for a long afternoon's climbing. **Routes:** 5 routes. One route, Brown Argus, up the obvious flake left of the arête was climbed in the 1960's though not recorded according to local climber Malc Baxter. **Parking and approach:** A track leaves the A628T on its south side to the Woodhead tunnels to ample parking overlooking the juvenile River Etherow. The rocks are reached by crossing the bridge and then walking back along the river, crossing the Black Clough ford after 0.5km and following the shooting track, carrying straight on when the track turns right up the hill. Continue along the grass track for 200m heading for the quarry visible further along the track. Time from car to crag: 15mins (dependent on the state of the ford, the crossing of which may cause some delay and added interest when in spate!). **Access:** The rocks are on CRoW land.

Routes are described from Left to Right. The belay for routes 1 to 3 is from the block on top; the belay for route 4 is probably best using runners on the first significant ledge at 5m. For route 5, use the large block adjacent to the tree. To descend, either scramble up the heather covered slope above the block above the arête and then descend on the right wing of the quarry, or alternatively, traverse rightwards along the top ledge to the more substantial birch tree in the corner and abseil.

1. Red Admiral E1 5c   2017

7m   The strenuous steep bulging wall starting just right of its left arête. Gain the jug at 3.5m, move diagonally right to the centre of the wall to micro friends and then the crux, moving up and left to better holds and an easing of the angle. Finish left of the tree.

Paul Durkin on first ascents of Red Admiral (E1 5c) and Grizzled Skipper (E1 5b)

2. Brown Argus Severe   1960's

7m   The obvious flake just left of the arête. Getting out at the top on the left can be tricky - alternatively traverse right just before the top and finish, a little more easily, as for the following route.

3. Peacock VS 4c   2016

7m   The wall just right of the arête finishing up the short groove and overhanging block above.

Simon Royston on first ascents of Peacock (VS 4c) & Common Hawker (E1 5b)

4. Common Hawker E1 5b 2016

7m Start left of the corner. From a side hold on the right, and if you're 6' 4", make a l-o-n-g reach to gain the ledge. If you don't measure up, a dyno is your only option. Make a step up before careful footwork gives a standing position on that first (so hard to reach) ledge. Move up more easily to stand on the large ledge below the top - belay here.

5. Grizzled Skipper E1 5b 2016

7m The steep wall starting 5m right of the corner. Take the right side of the overlap, making tricky moves to good holds on the wide ledge. Balance up to reach the cracks above and a standing position on the ledge - get your breath back, place solid runners and then head left and up to finish left of the small rowan tree. Large friend belay available in the block behind.

****

First Ascents

1960's   **Brown Argus** Malc Baxter (and possibly others)
4 Sept 2016   **Peacock** Simon Royston, Paul Durkin, Malc Baxter
11 Sept 2016 **Common Hawker** Simon Royston, Paul Durkin, Malc Baxter
18 Sept 2016 **Grizzled Skipper** Paul Durkin, Malc Baxter
23 April 2017 **Red Admiral** Paul Durkin, Simon Royston, Malc Baxter

24 Tintwistle Knarr Outcrop

Sam Whiting
OS ref. SK 035994 alt. 420m

An isolated buttress of excellent rock with great views. It wants to be more but isn't.

The 1843 OS map calls it Tintwistle Knarr, but that name is now given to the quarry some 1.25km east. Tintwistle Knarr quarry was originally called Millstone Rocks. Millstone Rocks is now identified 1km north-east at what is now (for climbers) called Lads Leap. Lads Leap is actually the crags near the top of Coombes Clough. Coombes Clough was also originally spelt Combs.

Interestingly, Laddow Rocks was originally called Ladder Rocks and the moor behind was called Ladder Moss.

Conditions and aspect: Lots of sun and clean. **Routes and bouldering:** Suited to bouldering for those who like a walk. Up to 5m high. Choose lines at will up to 5a. **Parking and approach:** As for Tintwistle Knarr Quarry or by paths from Tintwistle via Arnfield Brook. **Access:** No problems.

Sam Whiting enjoying some classic moorland grit

1. **My X** HVD
4m A nice little route, follow the crack up to a tricky finish.
2. **X Spand** S 4b
6m Up to the small pocket and reachy moves up the ripples to the top
3. **XIT** HVS 5a
6m Follow the vertical crack up to the ripples and pull over the top.
4. **X Pocket** HS 4a
6m Make a step up to the large pocket and some delicate moves to top.
5. **X Files** Diff
6m Easy moves up to the nose and from there a scamper up to the top.

First Ascents

The rock's been climbed on for years and first ascents cannot be attributed to anybody. However, thanks to Sam Whiting who recorded the five routes above in 2006.

25 Torside Naze

Malcolm Baxter
OS ref SK 072975   alt. 400m

Conditions and aspect: A very inconspicuous boulder that is actually a very small buttress which has tipped forward so that the top is a slab. It is on the moor edge above Long Gutter Edge and is between two fences. It is very isolated and there is nothing else anywhere near it. Its isolation and great scenery make it an esoteric tick but solitude should be the main attraction. Albeit small, the problems are worthwhile. It is also a rarely visited GPS cache. **Bouldering:** 8 problems.

Parking and approach: The approach (steep) is from the Torside pay and display car park at OS ref SK 068783. Time from car to crag: 30 - 40 mins.
Access: The rocks are on CRoW land.

26 Woodhead Tunnel Rocks

Paul Durkin
OS ref SK114999 alt. 280m

Conditions and aspect: Plenty of sun and suitable for dry winter days. The climbs are on rocks left by the railway tunnellers though somewhat defaced circa 2010 by the National Grid whilst placing HV cables into the adjacent disused tunnel - steel netting was placed over the crag fastened in place with 3 - 4m long rock anchors to control rock fall. Most of the netting's been removed but the anchors remain, leaving them as runners. The 5m deep vertical anchors at the top of the remaining netting also serve as belays. For most of the routes, careful scrambling up the netting is required to reach the belays. Alternatively, belay from the netting. **Routes:** 17 routes - some of the climbs were done jokingly but several turned out to be well worth a visit. **Parking and approach:** A track leaves the A628T on its south side to the Woodhead Tunnels to ample parking overlooking the River Etherow. The rocks are visible further along the track. Time from car to crag: 1min 20s. **Access:** The rocks are on CRoW land.

Routes are described from Left to Right

1.   Sleeper   VS 4c   1992
10m   Easy ledges to a narrow bottomless groove to a terrace. Spike belay.

2.   Wheeltapper   VS 5a   1992
10m   Strenuous initial moves up the overhanging nose on good holds before the final tricky arête, which is easier for the tall. Belay and abseil descent from the birch tree directly behind.

3.   The Fat Controller   VS 5a   1992
10m   The wall on the right to then take the arête of the previous route.

4.   Short-Ended Sleeper   VS 5b   2016
6m   Start directly below the rock anchor at a thin diagonal crack. Climb this to the ledge before moving up and right to the arête to reach the slot in the upper wall with a sequence of balance moves. Step left and up to the ledge avoiding any contact with the second rock anchor other than for a runner. Belay as for *Wheeltapper*.

5.   Axle Counter   HVS 5b *   2016
12m Easy climbing for 3m before scrambling up and left into the corner. Step right to the thin crack and climb it with the help of two pockets. At the ledge, exit right and up. For more interest the easy start can be replaced with the start to *The 7-11 to Eccles*.

6.   Guard's Van   VS 4c   2016
12m Start as for *Axle Counter* to the ledge and then ascend the flake directly in front of you, continuing on the left side of the arête.

7.   Colin Crompton's Bell   VS 4c   2016
12m A variation on *Guard's Van* though less satisfying. Start as the previous route as far as the second ledge. Continue on the right side of the arête/rib above.

8.   The 7-11 to Eccles   VS 5a   2016
11m Take the groove to a tricky exit at 4m. Move up and right at the ledge to ascend the front of the rib before easier ground is reached, trending right at the top.

Photo 26.1: Paul Durkin on first ascent of **Permanent Way**, E1 5b*

Source: Malcolm Baxter

9. Permanent Way   E1 5b *   2016
13m The centre of the overhanging wall to the small roof before attacking this to take the hanging arête just right directly onto the ledge. Catch your breath, shake out and continue easily, initially up the right side of the arête before finishing airily on its left side.

10. Shunter   VS 4c   2016
13m Start below the blunt arête and groove. Up this to the ledge and wide crack above to the second ledge before continuing up the rib and slab. The lower section can alternatively be taken at the same grade just right up the arête before rejoining at 2/3rds height.

11. Replacement Bus Service   HS 4b   2016
6m Start 1m right of the embedded bent steel bar and go straight up for the highest point of the wall.

12. Out of Your Signal Box   E2 5c *   1993
10m The short slab to then climb the strenuous blank wall by a letterbox.

13. New Year's Destination   VS 5a *   1992
10m The fine arête on its left side starting up the short slab. An alternative (easier) ascent at VS 4c can be made by moving to the right side of the arête at the ledge before moving back to the left after a couple of moves.

Photo 26.2: Malcolm Baxter, 1st ascent of **Out of Your Signal Box**, E2 5c*

14. PICOW Diff   2016
8m   Start 2m right of *New Year's Destination*, just right of a small corner. Make pleasing moves to the ledge at 2m - step up the slope to stand beneath the overhang. Climb it on its right at the weakness, step back left and continue more easily to the top.

15. Platform 9 VS 5a   2016
6m   Take the short wall before moving up and right onto the slab directly beneath the roof. Reach up and take the overhang directly just left of its nose. Feels scarier than it should.

16. Platform 9¾ VS 5a   2016
8m   Start as Platform 9 before moving right and up onto the slab. Traverse left beneath the overhang to make a balance move up and back right to the finish. If you step down onto the dirt ledge at the end of the leftward traverse to look for more protection only award yourself a HS tick.

17. End of the Line VS 5a   2016
6m   Start below the remains of the shot hole left of the large beak shaped rock. Climb up to achieve a standing position on the beak before attacking the upper section from the left to a finish which isn't as straightforward as it might appear.

First Ascents

31 Dec 1992 **Sleeper, Wheeltapper, The Fat Controller, New Year's Destination** Malcolm Baxter, Andy Gee, Dave French

The original ascent of New Year's Destination in 1992 at VS 4c used a large block which has since fallen out, leaving an improved slightly harder route. This and the easier right side variant were led by Royston on 30 May and 23 April 2016 respectively.

1 Jan 1993 **Out of Your Signal Box** Malcolm Baxter, David Hadfield

This ascent of an excellent route should be put into context, as according to Baxter - "It was very, very cold - at least minus two!"

10 April 2016 **Colin Crompton's Bell** Simon Royston, Paul Durkin, Malcolm Baxter

23 April 2016 **Permanent Way** Paul Durkin, Simon Royston, Malcolm Baxter

8 May 2016 **Shunter** Paul Durkin, Malcolm Baxter

5 June 2016 **The 7-11 to Eccles** Simon Royston, Paul Durkin, Malcolm Baxter

Platform 9¾ Malcolm Baxter, Simon Royston, Paul Durkin.

This original line climbed the initial short wall before moving up and left to reach a dirt ledge before the final balance move.

3 July 2016	**Axle Counter** Paul Durkin, Simon Royston, Malcolm Baxter
	Replacement Bus Service Simon Royston, Paul Durkin, Malcolm Baxter
17 July 2016	**Guard's Van, Platform 9¾** *(revised line)* Paul Durkin, Malcolm Baxter
	PICOW Malcolm Baxter, Paul Durkin
7 Aug 2016	**Short-Ended Sleeper** Simon Royston, Paul Durkin, Malcolm Baxter
	The line of Permanent Way *was also straightened out that day by Durkin to take the hanging arête above the start directly rather than traversing beneath it to the easier corner.*
14 Aug 2016	**Platform 9** Simon Royston, Paul Durkin, Malcolm Baxter
	End of the Line Paul Durkin, Simon Royston, Malcolm Baxter

27 Near Yellowslacks

Paul Durkin
OS refs SK055955 alt. 320m and SK060960   Alt.440m

This edge is for those who like a stiff uphill walk to warm you up followed by some good moorland rock with a brilliant view. There are two edges separated by about 1km - Lightside and Nat's Cabin.

The first edge encountered, Lightside, comprises two distinct buttresses about 50m apart, the first about 10m long and 4m high, the second about 30m and again 4m high. The buttresses are characterised by sharp edges and breaks with the occasional loose piece of rock - sometimes just where you don't want it!

The second edge, Nat's Cabin, is located northeast and comprises one large edge, 7m high and 15m, long and is hidden behind a shoulder off Harrop Moss and faces northeast at an altitude of 440m. The edge is similarly characterised by sharp edges and breaks.

Conditions and aspect: The first two buttresses face south-south-east and enjoys the sun for most of the day. The second higher buttress faces just south of east. **Routes and bouldering:** 25 routes from S to HVS. All the lines are boulder problems. **Parking and approach:** Vehicular access is from the A57 to Old Glossop, turning right to reach the bus turning circle - please park with consideration. Follow the unmade vehicle track north east until a field gate is reached. Turn left and go through the stile. Follow the path uphill to the boundary of open country is reached. Continue for a further mile until a small cairn can be seen on the right of the path. Turn 90° right about 50m before this - the first buttress is about 20m away, the second about 50m north east again. The second edge is reached by regaining the path and following it north eastwards for 1km. Pass over a stile, before leaving the main path on the left to follow a faint path up hill, veering leftwards when the edge can be seen. 45 minutes from car to the first climb. **Access:** The edge is on open moorland with no access restrictions.

The first isolated buttress at the left end

About 20m right are

The next buttress is some 150m right

Near Yellowslacks

The edge continues

Nat's Cabin Area

Kirklees Area

Raiding parties across the West Yorkshire border led to the inclusion of Holme Moss, Ramsden Edge, Whitegate Quarry, Marsden Clough and Bilberry Reservoir slabs within these pages. Marsden Clough is in outstanding surroundings and is a pleasure on a sunny day.

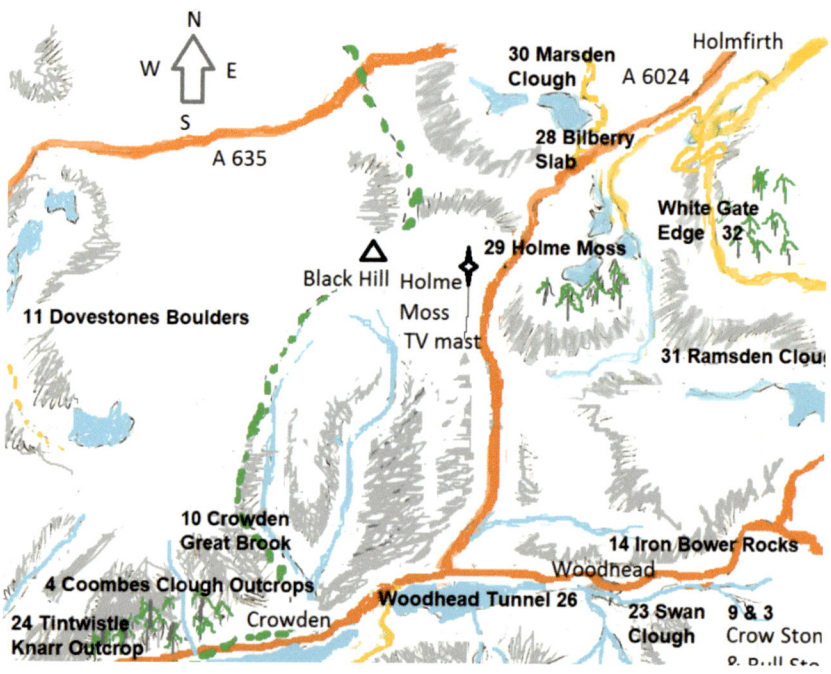

Map 27.1:   Kirklees Edges and Rocks

28 Bilberry Reservoir Slab

Paul Durkin
OS ref SE102070   alt. 265m

This slab was discovered by chance while returning from an exploration of Marsden Clough buttresses on the opposite side of the reservoir (see Chapter 30). The slab was originally covered in 'purest green' together with the more normal heather, moss, lichen and bilberry. A good day's climbing was unearthed over several months. The slab comprises an 11m high gritstone challenge characterised by smooth rock with the occasional patch of dodgy rock - not unexpected when you consider its been covered in wet vegetation for the last 100 years or so! The climbs vary in length from 6m to 15m. Good tree belays on the top.

Bilberry Reservoir is the second dam to be built on this spot - the first, an earth dam with a 20m high puddle clay core, collapsed catastrophically in 1852 causing 81 deaths in what became known as the Holmfirth flood.

Conditions and aspect: The edge faces north and only gets a few stray rays at the end of the day - good for those sweltering summer days - do you remember them! **Routes and bouldering:** 8 routes from Severe to E1. **Parking and approach:** From Digley Reservoir car park at SE109068 stay on the south side of the water and go west towards Bilberry Reservoir. Don't cross the dam wall - hop over the small concrete wall on the left and proceed on the bilberry and heather smothered berm for about 75m. Fifteen minutes from car to slab. **Access:** The slab is on water authority land and climbers have no right of access.

Bilberry Reservoir slab from the opposite side of the reservoir

1. Blueberry E1 5b — 2012
9m From the top of the large block make difficult moves to achieve a standing position on the left end of the flake (avoid using any holds on Snozzcumber). Continue with interest up the wall above.

2. Snozzcumber VS 4b — 2012
10m The left edge of the obvious flake - not technically hard but not for the faint hearted as protection is spaced.

3. Fraughan E1 5b * — 2012
11m Start 1m left of the arête to reach the first break using small ledges. Take one small step up, check the runners by your feet, and then make a difficult move (crux) up the slab to the break. If you put a side runner in the crack of *Ground Hurt*, only award yourself HVS.

4. Ground Hurt VS 5a * — 2012
15m The right side of the flake to reach the break. Move left until below the obvious crack which is followed to reach the next break. Move back right to the final crack.

5. Whortleberry HVS 5b — 2012
11m Make a hard move up and right from the right end of the block to reach the break. Step up and leftward, staying 1.5m left of the arête.

6.   Wimberry S 4b   2012
11m The crack line, passing the oak on its left. Continue up the right edge. A poor route after the initial moves.

7.   Myrtle 5a   2012
6m Make difficult moves to reach the break, reach over to good holds which enable the overhang to be conquered.

8.   Windberry 5a   2012
6m Step tentatively off the block to reach the wide break. Pull over the overhang onto the ledge above.

****

First Ascents

12 Aug 2012 **Ground Hurt** Malc Baxter and Simon Royston
1 Sept 2012 **Whortleberry** Paul Durkin, Simon Royston and Malc Baxter
             Fraughan (side runner in *Ground Hurt*), **Snozzcumber** Simon Royston, Paul Durkin and Malc Baxter.
15 Sept 2012 **Wimberry, Myrtle, Windberry, Fraughan** (no side runner) Paul Durkin, Simon Royston
             Blueberry Simon Royston, Paul Durkin

29 Holme Moss

Paul Durkin
OS ref SE098044   alt. 485m

A connoisseur's crag if ever there was one! An isolated crag which gives a pleasant half day's climbing. A single buttress on Kaye Edge overlooking the A6024 from Holme up to the Holme Moss radio mast. The climbs vary in height from 5m to 6m. Belays at the top are nowhere to be seen and have to be carried with you - cleaning and first ascents were made using steel spikes (now removed) driven into the ground behind the remains of the dry stone wall on top of the crag. Alternatively, just solo them.

Conditions and aspect: The edge faces south and east and gets the sun in the morning and early afternoon. **Routes and bouldering:** 6 routes from Diff to VS 5a. **Parking and approach:** From the car park at SE098039 cross the road and follow the access road towards the mast until you reach a gate on the right - sometimes locked. Follow the tyre tracks northwards for some 300m before veering north east until the remains of a dry-stone wall are reached on the escarpment edge. The buttress is some 15m further on. 15 minutes from the car park. **Access:** The edge is on access land.

1.   **Forks** VS 4c   2014
6m   Pull up at the left side to reach the large ledge and then make moves to stand on the same ledge before continuing up the wall above. Starting just right of the middle gives an alternative start at the same grade.

2.   Handlebars S 4a   2013
5m   The left edge of the slabby wall - not technically hard but enjoyable.

3.   Centre Cog VS 4c   2014
6m   Straight up the middle heading for the short crack at 2/3^{rds} height.

4.   Seat Post VS 4b   2014
6m   The right side of the slabby wall just left of the arête.

5.   Saddle Diff   2013
6m   Around the corner, the easy groove to the right of the arête.

6.   Derailleur VS 5a   2014
6m   Step onto the wide ledge from the right. Move up and back right to the centre of the wall, aiming for the short vertical crack before an awkward finish.

****

First Ascents

10 Nov 2013   **Saddle** Malc Baxter, Simon Royston
              Handlebars Simon Royston solo
              Cleaned and climbed on one of the most miserable days imaginable - all done for the love of climbing!

18 May 2014   **Forks, Seat Post** Simon Royston, Paul Durkin
              Centre Cog, Derailleur Paul Durkin, Simon Royston
              By contrast one of the nicest days of the year where shorts even made an appearance. With the Tour de France only a few weeks away the adjacent A6024 was awash with bikes making the horribly steep ascent. In recognition of all the expended effort the climbs have been named for their sport.

30 Marsden Clough

Paul Durkin
OS ref SE095073   alt. 285m

A delightfully isolated crag which gives a good day's climbing and delivers more than it appears to offer. It comprises two moorland gritstone buttresses separated by some 30m, characterised by rough rock and steep faces. The climbs vary in height from 5m to 8m. Good belays can be found on top and in the areas behind the main rocks.

Conditions and aspect: The edge faces south and gets the sun all day. **Routes and bouldering:** 16 routes from Diff to E1. **Parking and approach:** From the southern Digley Reservoir car park at SE109068 stay on the south side of the water and go west towards Bilberry Dam. Cross the dam wall and take the track adjacent to the north side of Bilberry Reservoir continuing straight on where the track doubles back on itself, crossing a fence to do so. Continue for 150m or so. Twenty minutes from car to crags. **Access:** The edge is on water authority land and climbers have no right of access.

Marsden Clough before cleaning

Nasal Buttress
1.   **Eustachian** VS 4c   2012
5m   The wall direct.
2.   **The Nose** VS 4c   2012
6m   Starting below the obvious corner climb into it, onto the arête on the right, and then the top (which presents its own challenge!).
3.   **Septum** V Diff   2012
6m   The corner to the right using the fin of rock and left wall.
4.   **Nose Hair** S   2012
6m   Chimney up the right side of the fin to the off width top crack.

5.   Sinus Trouble VS 5a   2012
5m   Just right of the corner take the middle of the slab and then directly over the roof and up the wall without using the arêtes.

6.   Sniffle Wall E1 5b *   2012
7m   Looks easy but isn't! Step off the banking onto the lower ledge, traverse right to the arête before making difficult moves to attain the pocket in the middle of the wall from where the difficulties ease.

7.   Rana E1 5c   2012
7m   Step off the block onto the arête. Move onto the front and climb the overhanging arête on its right. Seems easy doesn't it? **Rana Direct** - a 5c direct start is possible up the arête (6a if you're less than 1.8m tall).

8.   S'not Bad HVS 5b *   2012
8m   The small hanging arête on the LHS of the face to a good hold on the right. Pull over and onto the face before making a tricky step right onto the block and the large ledges above.

9.   E.N.T. E1 5b   2012
8m   From under the overhang reach good holds before launching up and left, then head right and up. Take the wall and crack above direct.

10.   Sneeze VS 4c   2012
7m   Take the overhanging crack and wall above.

11. My Cat Has No Nose VS 4c   2012
7m   The arête on its right side to the ledge before taking the wall above (see if you can spot the cats eyes in the top wall). An alternative start goes directly up the overhanging wall just left of the arête at 5a.

Moving 30m right to the next buttress

Tumbledown Buttress

12. Sphenoid VS 4c   2012
5m   A tricky layback leads to easier ground.

13. Tissues HS 4b   2012
6m   Make a hard(ish) move up the bottom block, make a move up the corner before traversing left to finish up the short crack.

14. Gremlin's Nose HVS 5b   2012
6m   The next lower corner right of *Tissues* to reach the same corner before making a hard move onto the nose to pull over the overhang.

15. Dew Drop Diff   2012
5m   Just right is a diagonal crack. Up this and the corners above.

16. Greensleeves VS 4c   2012
5m   The short wall to a ledge before making a step up and right.

First Ascents

22 July 2012	**S'not Bad**, **The Nose** Paul Durkin, Malc Baxter, Simon Royston
	Sniffle Wall Malc Baxter, Simon Royston, Paul Durkin
29 July 2012	**Sinus Trouble, Tissues** Paul Durkin, Adrienn Angyal, Simon Royston, Malc Baxter
	Sneeze, Nose Hair Paul Durkin solo
	Dew Drop Adrienn Angyal solo
	Septum Simon Royston solo
	My Cat Has No Nose, Greensleeves Simon Royston, Adrienn Angyal, Malc Baxter, Paul Durkin
	Gremlin's Nose Malc Baxter, Simon Royston, Adrienn Angyal and Paul Durkin
1 Sept 2012	**Sphenoid** Malc Baxter solo
9 Sept 2012	**Rana** Malc Baxter, Paul Durkin and Simon Royston
	Having top roped it first, Malc declared he could lead it - which was a good thing as we couldn't get near it! Both seconds admitted after following Malc to having 'a little bit of tension'. Nearly 72 and still beating the 'youngsters'.
	E.N.T. Simon Royston solo
7 Oct 2012	**Eustachian** Paul Durkin, Simon Royston and Malc Baxter
28 Apr 2013	**Rana Direct** (start only) Simon Royston, Paul Durkin both solo

Photo 30.1: Paul Durkin, **S'not Bad,** HVS 5b* first ascent, Marsden Clough

Source: Malcolm Baxter

31 Ramsden Clough

Paul Durkin
OS ref   SK122045   alt. 370m

The rocks are split into three distinct areas - a quarried bay, two quarried buttresses, and to the south east a natural edge. All have until recently been neglected (the first bay still has no climbs - when you see it, you'll see why!). The rock comprises sandy gritstone characterised by sharp edges with some unsound bands. The climbs vary in height from 5m to 12m.

Conditions and aspect: The bay and two buttresses face west and enjoy the afternoon sun. The higher southern edge faces northwest and hence receives only late afternoon/evening sun. Care needs to be taken with some of the tops which can be dusty and loose. **Routes and bouldering:** 26 routes from HVD to E2. **Parking and approach:** From the A6024, turn at Holmbridge into Bank Lane (at SK121068) which is followed into Brownhills Lane for approximately 1m to reach the car park above the dam at Ramsden Reservoir. Walk up the hill behind the car park and follow the footpath south skirting the tree line for approximately 1.5km until the first bay comes into view on the left - still waiting for a first ascent! The next two buttresses are 50m south. The higher southern edge is 200m southeast and some 50m higher. 35 minutes from car park to the quarry - another sweaty 15 minutes to the southern edge. For an alternative route park off the minor road next to the steel gate at SK131048. Follow the track for 10 minutes west past the peat diggings to the gas pipe marker at the corner of Crossley's plantation before turning south. Continue down the track for 5 minutes to where a 5m stretch of dry-stone wall points down the hill. Walk down the hill in the direction the wall points, cross the remains of another wall to a faint path heading northwest down the slope toward the end of another section of wall. Continue downwards right of the wall to reach the top of the first buttress where a path winds around the west side of it. Only 20 minutes from car to crag (the return trip up the hill takes a little longer!).
Access: The climbs are in the Peak District National Park in open countryside with no access restrictions.

Second Bay/Buttresses

Steel posts have been installed above the two faces to provide safe anchorages. The narrower left face - Broken Buttress - has a post some 3m back from the top. The bigger face - Broken Wall - has a substantial steel post embedded in the heather above the shale bank some 15m above the face. Climbs are described from left to right.

Broken Buttress

1. Blackpool Castaways E1 5a   2013
7m   A deceptive route with some interesting moves - a good route.

2. Heysham VS 4c   2012
8m   The wall with some interest. Alternatively, and slightly harder, start up the wall to the left.

3. Fleetwood HS   2010
9m   Parallel cracks to the niche and the left arête.

4. Morecambe HVS 5a   2010

10m Starting just right of the lowest point of the buttress ascend the slab and crack, passing a rusty steel 'blade' on the left, to the pedestal. Continue up the wall above.

5. Cassini's Destination E2 6a   2013

10m Follow Morecambe to the rusty steel blade. Move left to reach a side hold before making moves up and left (crux) to reach better holds in the crack. Go straight up the front of the stacked blocks.

6. Southport VS 4c   2012

10m Start below the arête and climb it! Spoilt a little by the step onto the grassy ledge at 4m.

Broken Wall

*Because of the nature of the rock, leading is **NOT** recommended on this wall, though fun can be had on a top rope.*

7. Hopscotch 5b   2011

12m Tricky moves to gain the ledge then more easily to the top. It's possible to exit leftwards after the lower wall.

8. Skittles 5c   2011

12m The lower wall to the ledge, then with increasing difficulty follow the groove/niche to the break and the top

9. Marbles 5b   2011

11m The crackline in the centre of the wall to a tricky finish (has been led but is not for those with a nervous disposition).

10. Conkers 6a   2011
10m The difficulties start at one-third height and continue for some time!
11. I Spy S 4b   2011
8m   The crack past the tree.

Southern Edge

12. Twins S 4b   2011
6m   Pleasantly up the corner using the two fist wide cracks.
13. Slippy Arête E2 5c   2011
7m   From the ledge at 3m achieve a standing position on the wall (crux).
14. Wobble Wall E2 5c   2011
7m   Stand on the projecting flake at 2m, from there, committing moves up the centre of the wall.
15. Affronted HS 4c   2011
6m   Easily between the two stone blocks to the wide crack which is harder than it appears.
16. Deceptive Bastard HVS 5c   2011
7m   Start below the steep crack in the overhanging wall. Easily up the first 2m and then the fun starts! The name says it all!

17. Legitimate Flake HS 4b   2011
7m   Just right is a fist wide crack at low level - up this and the final flake above.

18. Crack'n'Wall VS 5b   2011
7m   The wide crack to the ledge, an awkward move right and the hanging wall above.

19. Surprise Chimney VS 4c   2011
7m   The chimney, which is surprisingly good - honest!

20. You Can't be too Careful! HVS 5b   2011
7m   The crack in the lower wall (without using the earth bank) to attain a standing position on the ledge, crux. More easily up the wall above.

The next climbs are some 25m right, reached by crossing either the soggy ground at the bottom of the crag, or, better, cross the top of the crag and scrambling round the end and down.

21. Dodgy Hip HVS 5b   2011
5m   The middle of the wall without using the arêtes.

22. The Wrong Glasses (Again!) VS 5a   2011
5m   The centre of the wall until a move left enables a hard move up on small footholds and smaller finger holds. Straighten up and reach the welcome ledge. Probably 5c for the short.

23. Dusty VS 4b   2011
5m   The centre of the wall again, but move right from the ledge before ascending the wall - good.

24. Cam Corner HS 4c   2011
5m The layback crack in the corner.
25. Cracked Arête HS 4c   2011
6m Start to the left of the arête and climb the steep crack line.
26. Stroll Diff   2011
5m The right side of the arête - onto the projecting ledge and then use large holds and the hanging flake.

****

First Ascents

2010 March	**Fleetwood** Paul Durkin, Simon Royston	
	Morecambe Simon Royston, Malc Baxter, Paul Durkin	
2011 March	**Conkers** Simon Royston, Malcolm Baxter - top roped	
	I Spy Simon Royston, Malcolm Baxter, Paul Durkin	
2011 April	**Slippy Arête** Simon Royston, Paul Durkin - top roped	
	Hopscotch Simon Royston, Paul Durkin - both solo	
	Skittles Simon Royston - top roped	
	Marbles Paul Durkin, Simon Royston	
2011 June	**You Can't be too Careful!** Simon Royston, Paul Durkin, Malcolm Baxter	
	Twins Paul Durkin, Malcolm Baxter, Simon Royston	
	Affronted Malcolm Baxter, Paul Durkin, Simon Royston	
	Deceptive Bastard Paul Durkin, Simon Royston	
	Wobble Wall Simon Royston, Paul Durkin - top roped	
2011 July	**Dodgy Hip, Stroll** Paul Durkin solo	
	Dusty, Cam Corner, Cracked Arête, Legitimate Flake Paul Durkin, Malc Baxter	
	The Wrong Glasses (Again!) Paul Durkin, unseconded	
	Surprise Chimney Malc Baxter, Paul Durkin	
2011 Aug	**Heysham** Malc Baxter, Simon Royston. Alternate start Paul Durkin Oct 2013.	
	Southport Simon Royston, Malc Baxter	
2013 Oct	**Cassini's Destination** Malc Baxter	
	His seconds on the day could not follow him cleanly. Try this yourself when you're 73!	
	Blackpool Castaways Simon Royston, Malc Baxter, Paul Durkin	

32 White Gate Edge

Paul Durkin
OS ref SE130062   alt. 340m

Surprisingly this quarry has not been climbed in before, at least there's no record available, much to the delight of the author and first ascensionists. The crag top has been dug out and brushed so the climbs can be finished safely. Care is still needed with the tops as the rock exfoliates in plates. Five scaffold pole belays have been driven in along the top of the crag just in front of the dry-stone wall.

On a sunny day there isn't a better place to be than sitting back in the derelict quarry building sipping tea and watching hares running through the heather and a sparrow hawk skimming the contours. The quarry is a beginner's paradise - apart from the tops! There are a few harder routes as well,

Conditions and aspect: The quarry faces west and enjoys the sun from noon onwards. **Routes and bouldering:** 32 routes from Diff to E2. **Parking and approach:** Vehicular access is from White Gate Road. Park on the wide grass verge just before the junction with Woodhouse Lane. Walk back up the road for 80m and turn left onto a narrow track. Follow this past a turn off until a derelict quarry building is reached. The quarry is on the right. Three minutes from car to the quarry. **Access:** The edge is adjacent to farmland but currently there are no access restrictions. On Sunday mornings a clay pigeon shooting club use the adjacent quarry - when the red flag is flying keep your head off the right-hand skyline and beware sudden bangs and the fall of shattered clays!

Corbett's Wall

1. **Sooty** D 2011
5m The easy arête.
2. **Sweep** VD 2011
5.5m The crack 1m right.
3. **Kipper** S 4b 2011
6m The crack passing the left side of the cave.
4. **Butch** VS 5a 2011
6m An eliminate line - avoid the upper adjacent cracks - protection too!
5. **Soo** HS 4b 2011
6m An awkward start to reach the cave and another one to start the top wall.
6. **Maggie** VS 4c 2011
6m Start as for Soo then step right and follow the arête.

The long wall to the right, *Broadside Wall*, is home to 11 routes, only one of them harder than VS 5a.

7. **Yard Arm** VS 4c 2011
6m Start beneath and to the right of the small roof. Move up and left to the ledge and wall above.
8 **Gunpowder Groove** S 4b * 2011
6m The groove just right - nice!
9 **Grapeshot** VS 5a 2011
7m From beneath the crack line left of the undercut corner make a hard move to establish yourself on the wall, then go up and past the pocket.
10 **Magazine Crack** HS 4b 2011
7m 1m right the flaky wall and crack.
11 **Long Tom Wall** VS 5a 2011
6m Right again follow ledges straight up

| 12 | **Flintlock Wall** VS 5a | 2011 |

7m   An eliminate just left of *Gunport Groove* and left of the arête.

| 13 | **Gunport Groove** S 4b | 2011 |

7m   The vertical crack to the slanting groove and a challenging top.

| 14 | **Top Sail** VS 4c | 2011 |

6m   The wall between the groove and left side of the cave.

| 15 | **T'Gallant** S 4a | 2011 |

6m   The wall below the left end of the cave and the crack above it.

| 16 | **Mizzenmast** VS 4c | 2011 |

6m   Start directly below the right of the cave finishing left of the white lichen.

The Prow and the three routes to its right are all very good, overhanging and strenuous, and have good protection if you can hang on long enough.

17   The Prow E1 5b *   2011
Small edges to the ledge, balance right to the arête. Move up, a large Rock in the hole, and then make a long reach up and left to good holds. Move back right to the arête and the top.

18   Stay Sail HVS 5a   2013
7m   The left side of the steep wall just right of the arête
19   Bowsprit HVS 5b   2011
7m   The middle of the wall via finger locks at half height. Move right to the flake, make a difficult move to reach a solid hand jam and the top.
20   Flying Jib HVS 5a   2011
7m   Start as for the previous route moving right at the ledge to better holds and the top.
21   Crow's Nest VS 4b   2011
7m   Easily to the ledge, bridge up to the first runner! Make airy moves on good holds - much better than it looks.
22   Windlass VS 4c   2011
7m   The slab left of the arête and then up the steep blocks above.

Photo 32.1: Simon Royston on **Awesome Wells** E2 6a, first ascent

23   Awesome Wells E2 6a   2014

From half way up *Windlass* move right to a hold in the break. Make difficult strenuous moves to reach the horizontal break, where, after the quickest small cam placement ever, reach the hold high on the arête (it's not over yet!) and then make the top with a huge sigh of relief.

24   Porthole E1 5b *   2011
7m   Edges to reach the right side of the ledge. Make a committing move to reach the large slot. Up and left to a sloping strenuous top

25   Bow Wave VS 5a   2011
7m   The flake and wall below the upper wide crack to the ledge. Make an awkward move to get onto the arête and then the wide crack above.

Poets Wall Area

26   Coleridge's Crack VD   2011
8m   The obvious slanting crack in the corner.

27   Blake's Wall VS 4c   2011
8m   The wall 1.5m right (without using Coleridge's crack).

28   Donne's Dogleg HS 4b?   2011
8m   Start beneath the small dogleg crack and go straight up.

29   Austen's VD   2011
7m   Start beneath the hanging crack and guess what - go straight up! The wall to the right of the upper crack can also be climbed at 4c.

30   Eliot's Lightning Flash VD   2011
7m   The corner and arête to the upper crack and the belay ledge.

31   Graves' Wall E1 5c *   2011
6m   The middle of the wall on small edges to reach a thin finger hold at 5m before making a hard move up. Harder for those with fat fingers. Micro wedge required. If you use the large hold 1m left at 5m it's only 5b.

32   Hughes' Stroll D   2011
4m   Easily to the belay ledge.

A low level 5b traverse has been done across the whole quarry without using the large ledge which is at about 3.5m height except for the short length between Top Sail and Mizzenmast.

****

2011 Aug	**Hughes' Stroll** Simon Royston Solo
	Sooty Simon Royston Solo
	Sweep, Gunport Groove Paul Durkin Solo
	Long Tom Wall Simon Royston, Iain Johnson, Malc Baxter
	Gunpowder Groove Malc Baxter, Simon Royston
	Yard Arm Simon Royston, Malc Baxter
	Magazine Crack Iain Johnson, Malc Baxter, Simon Royston
	Kipper, T'Gallant, Flintlock Wall, Grapeshot Simon Royston, Paul Durkin, Malc Baxter
	Butch, Windlass, Bow Wave, Top Sail Paul Durkin, Malc Baxter, Simon Royston
	Soo, Mizzenmast Malc Baxter, Paul Durkin, Simon Royston
2011 Sept	**Coleridge's Crack, Blake's Wall, Donne's Dogleg** Simon Royston, Paul Durkin, Malc Baxter
	Austen's Malc Baxter, Paul Durkin
	Eliot's Lightning Flash Paul Durkin, Malc Baxter, Simon Royston
2011 Oct	**Graves' Wall, Maggie** Paul Durkin, Malc Baxter
	Flying Jib Malc Baxter, Paul Durkin
	Stay Sail Paul Durkin, Simon Royston, Malc Baxter *yo-yo ascent*. Led clean by Paul Durkin 10 August 2013.
	Bowsprit Paul Durkin, Simon Royston, Malc Baxter *yo-yo ascent*
	Crow's Nest Paul Durkin, Simon Royston, Malc Baxter

	The Prow Paul Durkin, Simon Royston, Malc Baxter
	Porthole Simon Royston, Paul Durkin, Malc Baxter
2014 Aug	**Awesome Wells** Simon Royston, Malc Baxter, Paul Durkin
	The route had been top roped in 2011 and we returned on 31 August 2014 to try again. After several rehearsals on a top rope by Royston, including a look at the gear required, the route was finally laid to rest.

That concludes the epistle according to us, leaving us with a warm glow and a feeling of a job well done. So...the hunt for the next obscure crag continues.....the gnome dances on!

Index

A

Acorner	20
Adri's Arête	66
Affronted	172
Africa Wall	26
Allegedly	14
Almost	37
Altar Crack	66
Another Wall	30
Aperitif	13
Arête and Wall	30
Audacity	33
Auntie Christine's Bran Cake	50
Austen's	180
Autumn Almanac	10
Awesome Wells	180
Axle Counter	149

B

Bar	141
Barling Royal Hunt	132
Bashful	8
Battle Axe	133
Battle of the Bulge	10
Beaky	76
Beast	66
Bête Blanche	56
Bête Noire	56
Betwixt and Between	10
Billet	141
Black & White	93
Black Edge	8
Black Edge Left Hand	8
Black Face	93
Black Fingers Wall	100
Blackpool Castaways	170
Blake's Wall	180
Bloodstain	93
Blueberry	160
Boulder Trundle	80
Bow Wave	180
Bowsprit	178
Brace and Bit	26
Braced and a Bit	22
Bradley's Hour	59
Brain Strain	101
Brevity	109
Bridge Too Far	57
Broken Arête	34
Brown Argus	143
Brown Wall	77
Brown(ian) Motion	119
Bruised	15
Bulge	76
Burning Daylight	54
Busky Buttress	66
Butch	176

C

Call of the Wild	53
Cam Corner	174
Cape Verde	26
Cassini's Destination	171
Caterpillar Crack	19
Caterpillar Rib	19
Caterpillar Wall	19
Catherine Wheel	13

Cave Route Left	30
Cave Route Right	30
Central	44
Centre Buckle	141
Centre Cog	163
Chorley or Eccles	52
Christmas Butterfly	53
Clamp	109
Clubs	12
Clutch	109
Cobnut Flake	132
Cold Steel	141
Coleridge's Crack	180
Colin Crompton's Bell	149
Common Hawker	144
Conkers	172
Cornerstone	109
Corsican Bandit	26
Crack and Block	39
Crack and Nose	32
Crack'n Corner	42
Crack'n Edge	22
Crack'n'Wall	173
Cracked Arête	174
Cracked Corner	49
Cracked Slab	49
Crackers	66
Cross Talk	67
Crossover	52
Crow's Nest	178
Crowless Foot	50
Crusader	57
Cure-All	101
Cutlass	83

D

D for Danger	33
Damocles' Boulders	15
Deadleg	26
Deadleg Crack	50

Death by Diamonds and Pearls	38
Deceptive Bastard	172
Deceptive LH	67
Deceptive RH	67
Derailleur	163
Dew Drop	166
Diamonds	12
Did I Offend Someone?	40
Dignity	109
Dionysius	15
Doc	8
Doctors Delight	101
Dodgy Hip	173
Donne's Dogleg	180
Double Edged	22
Dusty	173
Dyslexic	119

E

E.N.T.	165
Eadbut	95
Easy	35
Eccles Cake Wall	35
Elastic Modulus	141
Eliot's Lightning Flash	181
End of the Line	152
Entrée	13
Equal Angle	141
Escape	23
Eustachian	164

F

Figgly	124
Flakeless	34
Flaky Cracks	32
Flaky Pastry	40
Fleetwood	170
Flintlock Wall	177
Flying Jib	178
Footless	35

Footless Pigeon	50
Footloose	35
Forks	162
Foxglove	51
Fraughan	160
Freeborn Man	56
Frog's Mouth	23, 124
Fruit Slice Wall	35
Fruitcake	16
Frustrated	22
Fun in the Sun	57
Furry Crack	119

G

Gill Pot	125
Go On!	79
Gold Block	133
Gosh Josh	67
Gotcha	38
Grapeshot	176
Grassy Hole	80
Graves' Wall	181
Gravity	109
Green Corner	35
Green Fang	54
Green Fingers	79
Green Step	77
Green Wall	30
Greensleeves	166
Gremlin's Nose	166
Gripply	124
Grizzled Skipper	144
Ground Hurt	160
Grumpy	8
Guard's Van	149
Guinea Gold	132
Gunport Groove	177
Gunpowder Groove	176

H

Handlebars	163
Hanging Around	79
Hearts	12
Heysham	170
Hidden Wall	34
High Stepper	80
Hole in the Wall	42
Hollow Flake	16
Hopscotch	171
Hughes' Stroll	181
Hurricane	55

I

I Spy	172

J

Jagged Edge	119
Jammer	119
Jiggly	123
Jihad	55
Johnathon Livingstone Steel Fingers	71
Jouster	58
Judge Jeffreys	119
Juggler	132
Just About	38
Just Desert	13

K

Kipper	176
Kylie	16

L

L Climb	67
Lanyard	134
Lapwing	83
Left(ish) Wall	32
Legitimate Flake	173

Legover	93
Less Fir Tree Wall	38
Let's be Blunt	34
Letterbox Crack	11
Linnet	83
Literate	119
Litter Arête	119
Little Fir Tree Wall	38
Lola	11
Lonesome	126
Long Buttress	13
Long Tom Wall	176

M

Mace	83
Magazine Crack	176
Maggie	176
Magic Bramble	12
Marbles	171
Mein Kampf	54
Mental Mantels	57
Merlin	83
Messenger's Destination	66
Mizzenmast	177
Monster Mantels	52
Mop Up	109
Morecambe	171
My Cat Has No Nose	166
My X	146
Myrtle	161

N

Nearly	37
Nearly a Slab	23
New Year's Destination	151
No Country for Old Men	55
No Need for a Struggle	55
No Trumps	13
Nobut	95
Nose Hair	164

Nostril	31
Not For T'Short	42
NoTime for New Tricks	55

O

Oak Quest	120
Off-Hand	109
Ogden's Nut Gone Flake	132
On Site	51
Only Just	38
Oroxylum Indicum	16
Out of Your Signal Box	151

P

Parta the Strata	11
Paul's Wall	66
Peacock	143
Pedestal	77
Penumbra	45
Permanent Way	151
Pet Project	42
Peveril the Poisoner	58
PICOW	152
Piece of Cake	23
Pierrepoint	119
Pillar	67
Pint Pot	125
Pinwheel	13
Platform 9	152
Platform 9¾	152
Pluto	9
Pocket Wall	42
Port Side	83
Porthole	180
Portside Arête	30
Postman's Craic	11
Powdered Penguin	42
Private Parade	35
Proper Clean	52
Pure Green	119

Q

Quality Street	9
Quart Pot	125

R

Rana	165
Rana Direct	165
Ranger's Return	11
Rank and Vile	50
Red Admiral	143
Redbreast	132
Replacement Bus Service	151
Reservoir Dog	53
Right(ish) Wall	32
Right-Hand	109
Ripoff	109
Robin	136
Rope	119
Rough Shag	136
Rowan Wall	44
Rowan's Shade	45

S

S Climb	38
S'not Bad	165
Saddle	163
Saladin	59
Sandstorm	14
Satisfaction Guaranteed	10
Seat Post	163
Septum	164
Shield	83
Short Ended Sleeper	148
Short Wall	30
Shunter	151
Sicily	26
Sidewinder	49
Simon's Step	67
Simple Fare	13
Sinus Trouble	165
Six Steps to Heaven	57
Skinned	120
Skittles	171
Slant	22
Sleeper	148
Sleepy	8
Slippy Arête	172
Sneaky	51
Sneeze	165
Sneezy	8
Sniffle Wall	165
Snozzcumber	160
Soo	176
Sooty	176
Southport	171
Spades	12
Sphenoid	166
Spike Arête	10
St. Bruno	133
St. Julien	132
Stacked Arête	14
Staircase	31
Starboard Arête	30
Starter	22
Stay Sail	178
Step Up	22
Straight Talk	67
Stroll	174
Summer at Last?	44
Sunny Delight	12
Sunstroke	17
Super Trooper	50
Surety	119
Surfeit of Cakes	53
Surgeon's Stitch-Up	66
Surprise	49
Surprise Chimney	173
Swastika	55
Sweep	176

Index

Syracuse	15

T

T'Gallant	177
Tall Man's Arête	14
Teeterer	79
Tempter	79
That Crack Up There!	38
The 7-11 to Eccles	149
The Fat Controller	148
The Hole Thing	34
The Middle of the Blur	38
The Niche	35
The Nose (Ironbower)	109
The Nose (Marsden Clough)	164
The Prow	178
The Scariest	121
The Shelf	32
The Snark	51
The Stretch	44
The Summertime Blues	57
The Sundog	51
The Third Half	9
The White Face	93
The Wrong Glasses (Again!)	173
Thread Arête	40
Three Happy Ducks	20
Three Thousand Pounds!	45
Tissues	166
Toad's Mouth	23
Top Pocket	128
Top Sail	177
Topology	110
Tottering Tower	7
Trepidation	80
Twilight Quickstep	59
Twins	172
Two Up, One Across	67

U

Ummayyad	58
Uncertain	119
Uranus	9

V

Variety Crack	41
Very Flaky	42

W

Wall	22
Wall Like	22
Walnut Plug	135
Walnut Slice	135
Warm Up	22
Watch Out!	23
Waterloo Sunset	10
We're Jammin'	44
Wedding Anniversary	53
Wedge Wall	23
Wheeltapper	148
Where's That Oak Gone!	120
White Flakes	41
Whortleberry	160
Wiggly	124
Wimberry	161
Wimper & Cringe	20
Wind and Piss	34
Windberry	161
Windjammer	34
Windlass	178
Wobble Wall	172
Wren's Corner	9

X

X Files	146
X Pocket	146
X Spand	146
XIT	146

Y

Yard Arm	176
Yardarm	83
Yeabut	95
Yellow Peril	67
Yellow Wall	8
Yellow Wall Right-Hand	9
Yeti	119
You Can't be too Careful!	173

Z

Zeitgeist	124